DK EYEWITNESS TRAVEL

15-MINUTE
ITALIAN

DK EYEWITNESS TRAVEL

15-MINUTE
ITALIAN

LEARN ITALIAN
IN JUST 15
MINUTES A DAY

FRANCESCA LOGI

London, New York, Munich, Melbourne,
and Delhi

Dorling Kindersley Limited
Senior Editor Angeles Gavira
Project Art Editor Vanessa Marr
DTP Designer John Goldsmid
Production Controller Luca Frassinetti
Publishing Manager Liz Wheeler
Managing Art Editor Philip Ormerod
Publishing Director Jonathan Metcalf
Art Director Bryn Walls

Language content for Dorling Kindersley by
g-and-w publishing

Produced for Dorling Kindersley by
Schermuly Design Co.
Art Editor Hugh Schermuly
Project Editor Cathy Meeus
Special photography Mike Good

First American Edition, 2005

Published in the United States by
DK Publishing, Inc., 375 Hudson Street,
New York, New York 10014

05 06 07 08 09   10 9 8 7 6 5 4 3 2 1

A Cataloging-in-Publication record for this book
is available from the Library of Congress.

ISBN 0-7566-0924-0

15-Minute Italian is also available in a pack
with two CDs (ISBN 0-7566-0929-1)

Color reproduction by Colourscan, Singapore
Printed and bound in China by Leo Paper
Products Limited

Discover more at
www.dk.com

Contents

How to use this book   6

Week 1
Introductions

Hello   8
Relatives   10
My family   12
To be and to have   14
Review and repeat   16

Week 2
Eating and drinking

In the café   18
In the restaurant   20
To want   22
Dishes   24
Review and repeat   26

Week 3
Making arrangements

Days and months   28
Time and numbers   30
Appointments   32
On the telephone   34
Review and repeat   36

Week 4
Travel

At the ticket office   38
To go and to take   40
Taxi, bus, and metro   42
On the road   44
Review and repeat   46

Week 5
Getting around

Around town	48
Finding your way	50
Sightseeing	52
At the airport	54
Review and repeat	56

Week 6
Accommodation

Booking a room	58
In the hotel	60
At the campground	62
Descriptions	64
Review and repeat	66

Week 7
Shopping

Shops	68
At the market	70
At the supermarket	72
Clothes and shoes	74
Review and repeat	76

Week 8
Work and study

Jobs	78
The office	80
Academic world	82
In business	84
Review and repeat	86

Week 9
Health

At the pharmacy	88
The body	90
At the doctor	92
At the hospital	94
Review and repeat	96

Week 10
At home

At home	98
In the house	100
The backyard	102
Pets	104
Review and repeat	106

Week 11
Services

Mail and bank	108
Services	110
To come	112
Police and crime	114
Review and repeat	116

Week 12
Leisure and socializing

Leisure time	118
Sports and hobbies	120
Socializing	122
Review and repeat	124

Reinforce and progress	126
Menu guide	128
English–Italian dictionary	134
Italian–English dictionary	146
Acknowledgments	160

How to use this book

This main part of the book is devoted to 12 themed chapters, broken down into five 15-minute daily lessons, the last of which is a revision lesson. So, in just 12 weeks you will have completed the course. A concluding reference section contains a menu guide and English-to-Italian and Italian-to-English dictionaries.

Warm up and clock

Each day starts with a one-minute warm-up that encourages you to recall vocabulary or phrases you have learned previously. A clock to the right of the heading bar indicates the amount of time you are expected to spend on each exercise.

Instructions

Each exercise is numbered and introduced by instructions that explain what to do. In some cases additional information is given about the language point being covered.

Cultural/Conversational tip

These panels provide additional insights into life in Italy and language usage.

Text styles

Distinctive text styles differentiate Italian and English, and the pronunciation guide (see right).

In conversation

Illustrated dialogues reflecting how vocabulary and phrases are used in everyday situations appear throughout the book.

How to use the flap

The book's cover flaps allow you to conceal the Italian so that you can test whether you have remembered correctly.

Revision pages

A recap of selected elements of previous lessons helps to reinforce your knowledge.

Pronunciation guide

Many Italian sounds will already be familiar to you, but a few require special attention. Take note of how these letters are pronounced:

c   an Italian **c** is pronounced *ch* before **i** or **e** but *k* before other vowels: **cappuccino** kappoo*cheenoh*

ch   pronounced *k* as in <u>keep</u>

g   pronounced *j* as in <u>jam</u> before **i** or **e** but *g* as in <u>get</u> before other vowels

gh   pronounced *g* as in <u>go</u>

gn   pronounced *ny* like the sound in the middle of <u>onion</u>

gli pronounced *ly* like the sound in the middle of <u>million</u>

h   **h** is always silent: **ho** oh (*I have*)

r   an Italian **r** is trilled like a Scottish *r*

s   an Italian **s** can be pronounced either *s* as in <u>see</u> or *z* as in <u>zoo</u>

sc   pronounced *sh* as in <u>ship</u> before **i** or **e** but *sk* as in <u>skip</u> before other vowels

z   an Italian **z** is pronounced *ts* as in <u>pets</u>

Italian vowels tend to be pronounced longer than their English equivalents, especially:

e   as the English <u>lay</u>

i   as the English <u>keep</u>

u   as the English <u>boot</u>

After each word or phrase you will find a pronunciation transcription. Read this, bearing in mind the tips above, and you will achieve a comprehensible result. But remember that the transcription can only ever be an approximation and that there is no real substitute for listening to and mimicking native speakers.

Useful phrases
Selected phrases relevant to the topic help you speak and understand.

Say it
In these exercises you are asked to apply what you have learned using different vocabulary.

5   Say it

Do you have a single room, please?

For six nights.

Is breakfast included?

Dictionary
A mini-dictionary provides ready reference from English to Italian and Italian to English for 2,500 words.

Menu guide
Use this guide as a reference for food terminology and popular Italian dishes.

1 Warm up

The Warm Up panel appears at the beginning of each topic. Use it to reinforce what you have already learned and to prepare yourself for moving ahead with the new subject.

Buongiorno
Hello

In Italy a firm handshake usually accompanies an introduction or meeting in a formal situation. Italians greet relatives and friends with a kiss on each cheek but only when they haven't met, or are not going to see each other, for a while. Men often greet each other with a hug.

2 Words to remember

Say these polite expressions aloud. Hide the text on the left with the cover flap and try to remember the Italian for each. Check your answers and repeat, if necessary.

Ciao! chow	*Hi!*
Buongiorno. bwonjornoh	*Hello/Good day.*
Piacere. peeahcheray	*Pleased to meet you.*
Come si chiama? komay see keeamah	*What's your name?*
Buonasera/Buonanotte. bwonasayrah/ bwonanottay	*Good evening/ Good night.*

▮▮ Conversational tip Italians tend to use "sir" (signore), "madam" (signora), and "miss" (signorina) more than English-speakers would. These titles are also used with last names.

3 In conversation: formal

Buongiorno. Mi chiamo Suzi Lee.
bwonjornoh. mee keeamoh soozee lee

Hello. My name is Suzi Lee.

Buongiorno. Marco Paoletti, piacere.
bwonjornoh. markoh pa-olettee, peeahcheray

Hello. Marco Paoletti, pleased to meet you.

Piacere.
peeahcheray

Pleased to meet you.

4 Put into practice

Join in this conversation. Read the Italian beside the pictures on the left and then follow the instructions to make your reply. Then test yourself by concealing the answers with the cover flap.

Buonasera.
bwonasayrah
Good evening.

Say: *Good evening, madam.*

Buonasera signora.
bwonasayrah
seennyorah

Mi chiamo Marta.
mee keeamoh martah
My name is Marta.

Say: *Pleased to meet you.*

Piacere.
peeahcheray

5 Useful phrases

Familiarize yourself with these phrases. Read them aloud several times and try to memorize them. Hide the Italian with the cover flap and test yourself.

Goodbye.	**Arrivederci.** arreevederchee
See you soon.	**A presto.** ah prestoh
See you tomorrow.	**A domani.** ah domanee
Thank you.	**Grazie.** gratseeay

6 In conversation: informal

Allora, a domani?
allorah, ah domanee

So, see you tomorrow?

Sì, arrivederci a domani.
see, arreevederchee ah domanee

Yes, goodbye, see you tomorrow.

Arrivederci. A presto.
arreevederchee. ah prestoh

Goodbye. See you soon.

1 Warm up

Say "hello" and "goodbye" in Italian. (pp.8–9)

Now say "My name is…". (pp.8–9)

Say "sir" and "madam." (pp.8–9)

I parenti
Relatives

In Italian the word for *the* varies depending on whether the word it refers to is masculine or feminine—for example, **il cellulare** (*cell phone*) is masculine, but **la riunione** (*meeting*) is feminine. You will sometimes find **lo** used with masculine words. **Il**, **la**, and **lo** change to **l'** before a vowel.

2 Match and repeat

Look at the numbered family members in this scene and match them with the vocabulary list at the side. Read the Italian words aloud. Now, hide the list with the cover flap and test yourself.

1 **la sorella**
  lah sorellah

2 **il nonno**
  eel nonnoh

3 **il padre**
  eel padray

4 **il fratello**
  eel fratelloh

5 **la nonna**
  lah nonnah

6 **la figlia**
  lah feelyah

7 **la madre**
  lah madray

8 **il figlio**
  eel feelyoh

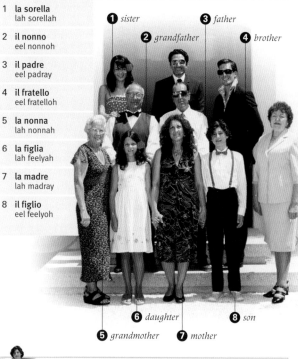

❶ *sister*　❸ *father*

❷ *grandfather*　❹ *brother*

❺ *grandmother*　❻ *daughter*　❼ *mother*　❽ *son*

Conversational tip In Italian the word "nipote" means four different things: nephew, niece, grandson, and granddaughter. For nephew and grandson you use the masculine "il nipote"; for niece and granddaughter you use the feminine "la nipote."

3 Words to remember: relatives

Look at these words and say them aloud. Hide the text on the right with the cover flap and try to remember the Italian. Check your answers and repeat, if necessary. Then practice the phrases below.

il marito
eel
mareetoh
husband

la moglie
lah molyay
wife

Sono sposato/sposata.
sono spozatoh/spozatah
I'm married (male/female).

uncle	**lo zio** loh tzeeoh
aunt	**la zia** lah tzeeah
cousin	**il cugino/la cugina** eel koojeenoh/lah koojeenah
in-laws	**i suoceri** ee swocheree
I have four children.	**Ho quattro figli.** oh kwattroh feelyee
We have two daughters.	**Abbiamo due figlie.** abbeeahmoh dooay feelyeeay
I have a sister.	**Ho una sorella.** oh oonah sorellah
I have two brothers.	**Ho due fratelli.** oh dooay fratellee

4 Words to remember: numbers

Memorize these words and then test yourself using the cover flap.

The word for "a" or "one" changes to match gender: **un fratello** (*a brother*, masculine); **una sorella** (*a sister*, feminine). **Un** changes to **uno** in front of "z" or "s" plus consonant: **uno zio** (*an uncle*), **uno sport** (*a sport*). **Una** changes to **un'** before a vowel: **un'amica** (*a female friend*). To make a plural a final "a" usually changes to "e": **figlia/figlie** (*daughter/daughters*). A final "o" or "e" usually changes to "i": **fratello/fratelli** (*brother/brothers*). "The" also changes in the plural: **le** for the feminine; **i** or **gli** for the masculine.

one	**uno** oonoh
two	**due** dooay
three	**tre** tray
four	**quattro** kwattroh
five	**cinque** cheenkway
six	**sei** say
seven	**sette** settay
eight	**otto** ottoh
nine	**nove** novay
ten	**dieci** deeaychee

Say the Italian for as
many members of the
family as you can.
(pp.10–11)

Say "I have two sons."
(pp.10–11)

La mia famiglia
My family

There are two ways of saying "you" in
Italian: formally and informally. **Lei** is
the formal version and **tu** is for family,
friends, and young people. This means
there are also different words for
"your"(see below). It's a good idea to
use the formal version until you are
addressed by the other person as **tu**.

2 Words to remember

There are different words for "my" and "your" in Italian, depending
on whether they precede a masculine, feminine, or plural word.

mio/mia mee-oh/me-eah	*my (masculine/ feminine singular)*
miei/mie mee-ayee/mee-ay	*my (masculine/ feminine plural)*
tuo/tua too-oh/too-ah	*your (informal masculine/feminine singular)*
tuoi/tue too-oh-ee/too-ay	*your (informal masculine/feminine plural)*
suo/sua soo-oh/soo-ah	*your (formal masculine/feminine singular)*
suoi/sue soo-oh-ee/soo-ay	*your (formal masculine/feminine plural)*

**Questi sono i miei
genitori.**
kwaystee sonoh ee
mee-ayee jeneetoree
These are my parents.

3 In conversation

Lei ha figli?
lay ah fillyee

*Do you have any
children?*

Sì, ho due figlie.
see, oh dooay feellyay

*Yes, I have two
daughters.*

**Queste sono le mie
figlie. E Lei?**
kwestay sonoh lay mee-
ay feellyay. ay lay

*These are my
daughters. And you?*

Conversational tip The Italians generally ask a question by simply raising the pitch of the voice at the end of the statement: "Vuole un po' di vino?" (Do you want a little wine?). Some questions are introduced by a question word (what, where, how, and so on): "Quant'è?" (How much is it?), "Dove va?" (Where are you going?).

4 **Useful phrases**

Read these phrases aloud several times and try to memorize them. Conceal the Italian with the cover flap and test yourself.

Do you have any brothers? (informal)	**Hai fratelli?** ahee fratellee
Do you have any brothers? (formal)	**Ha fratelli?** ah fratellee
This is my husband.	**Questo è mio marito.** kwestoh ay mee-oh mareetoh
This is my wife.	**Questa è mia moglie.** kwestah ay mee-ah molyay
Is that your sister? (informal)	**Quella è tua sorella?** kwellah ay too-ah sorellah
Is that your sister? (formal)	**Quella è sua sorella?** kwellah ay soo-ah sorellah

No, ma ho un nipote.
noh, mah oh oon neepotay

No, but I have a nephew.

5 **Say it**

Do you have any brothers and sisters? (formal)

Do you have any children? (informal)

I have two sisters.

This is my wife.

1 Warm up

Say "See you soon."
(pp.8–9)

Say "I am married"
(pp.10–11) and
"This is my wife."
(pp.12–13)

Essere e avere
To be and to have

There are some essential verbs that
you can use to make a range of useful
expressions. The first of these are
essere (*to be*) and **avere** (*to have*). In
Italian the verb form varies according
to the pronoun (I, you, he, she, and
so on). The pronoun itself is often
omitted, as it is implied by the verb.

2 Essere: to be

Familiarize yourself with the different forms of **essere** (*to be*) and, when
you are confident, practice the sentences below. Note that descriptive
words can have different endings depending on what is being described.

(io) sono (ee-oh) sonoh	*I am*
(tu) sei (too) say	*you are* *(informal singular)*
(Lei) è (lay) ay	*you are* *(formal singular)*
(lui/lei) è (loo-ee/lay) ay	*he/she/it is*
(noi) siamo (noy) see-ahmoh	*we are*
(voi) siete (voy) see-aytay	*you are* *(plural)*
(loro) sono (loroh) sonoh	*they are*

Sono inglese.
sonoh eenglesay
I'm English.

Di dov'è?/Di dove sei? dee dovay/dee dovay say	*Where are you from?* *(formal/informal)*
Siete in orario. see-aytay een orareeoh	*You're on time.*
È contenta? ay kontayntah	*Is she happy?*
Siamo italiani. see-ahmoh eetahleeahnee	*We're Italian.*

3 Avere: to have

Practice **avere** (*to have*) and the sample sentences, then test yourself.

I have	**(io) ho** (eeoh) oh
you have *(informal singular)*	**(tu) hai** (too) ahee
you have *(formal singular)*	**(Lei) ha** (lay) ah
he/she/it has	**(lui/lei) ha** (loo-ee/lay) ah
we have	**(noi) abbiamo** (noy) abbeeahmoh
you have (plural)	**(voi) avete** (voy) avetay
they have	**(loro) hanno** (loroh) annoh

Ha dei broccoli?
ah day brokkolee
Do you have
any broccoli?

Marco has a meeting.	**Marco ha una riunione.** markoh ah oonah reeooneeonay
Do you have a cell phone?	**Ha un cellulare?** ah oon chaylloolaray
How many brothers and sisters do you have?	**Quanti fratelli ha?** kwantee fratellee ah

4 Negatives

It is easy to make sentences negative in Italian. Just put **non** in front of the verb: **non siamo inglesi** (*we're not English*), **non ho fratelli** (*I don't have any brothers*).

la bicicletta
lah beecheeklettah
bicycle

He's not married.	**Non è sposato.** non ay spozatoh
I'm not sure.	**Non sono sicuro/a.** non sonoh seekooroh/ah
We don't have any children.	**Non abbiamo figli.** non abbeeamoh feelyee

Non ho l'auto.
non oh la-ootoh
I don't have a car.

Ripassa e ripeti
Review and repeat

1 How many?

1 **tre**
tray

2 **nove**
novay

3 **quattro**
kwattroh

4 **due**
dooay

5 **otto**
ottoh

6 **dieci**
deeaychee

7 **cinque**
cheenkway

8 **sette**
settay

9 **sei**
say

1 How many?

Hide the answers with the cover flap. Then say these Italian numbers aloud. Check to see if you remembered the Italian correctly.

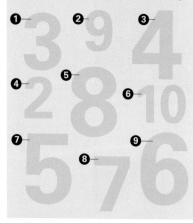

2 Hello

1 **Buonasera, mi chiamo...**
bwonasayrah, mee keeamoh...

2 **Piacere.**
peeahcheray

3 **Sì sono sposato/a, e ho due figli. E Lei?**
see sonoh spozatoh/ah, ay oh dooay feelyee. ay lay

4 **Arrivederci a domani.**
arreevederchee ah domanee

2 Hello

You meet someone in a formal situation. Join in the conversation, replying in Italian following the English prompts.

Buonasera, mi chiamo Suzi.
1 *Answer the greeting and give your name.*

Questo è mio marito, Piero.
2 *Say "Pleased to meet you."*

Lei è sposato/a?
3 *Say "Yes, I'm married and I have two sons. And you?"*

Noi abbiamo tre figlie.
4 *Say "Goodbye. See you tomorrow."*

3 To have or to be

Fill in the blanks with the correct form of **avere** (*to have*) or **essere** (*to be*). Check to see if you remembered the Italian correctly.

1 (io) _____ sposato/a.

2 (noi) _____ quattro figli.

3 (lei) _____ inglese.

4 (Lei) _____ un fratello?

5 (voi) _____ figli?

6 (io) non _____ il cellulare.

7 (tu) _____ sicuro.

8 (noi) _____ italiani.

3 To have or be

1 **sono**
   sonoh

2 **abbiamo**
   abbeeahmoh

3 **è**
   ay

4 **ha**
   ah

5 **avete**
   avetay

6 **ho**
   oh

7 **sei**
   say

8 **siamo**
   see-ahmoh

4 Family

Say the Italian for each of the numbered family members. Check to see if you remembered the Italian correctly.

❶ *sister*
❷ *grandfather*
❸ *father*
❹ *brother*
❺ *grandmother*
❻ *daughter*
❼ *mother*
❽ *son*

4 Family

1 **la sorella**
   lah sorellah

2 **il nonno**
   eel nonnoh

3 **il padre**
   eel padray

4 **il fratello**
   eel fratelloh

5 **la nonna**
   lah nonnah

6 **la figlia**
   lah feelyah

7 **la madre**
   lah madray

8 **il figlio**
   eel feelyoh

Al bar
In the café

Count up to ten.
(pp.10–11)

Remind yourself how
to say "hello" and
"goodbye." (pp.8–9)

Ask "do you have
a cell phone?"
(pp.14–15)

In a typical café-bar you can either
stand at the counter or sit at a table
with waiter service, which can be
more expensive. You can have a
variety of soft or alcoholic drinks. The
standard coffee is an **espresso**, a small,
black coffee. You can also order
pastries, sandwiches, and other snacks.

Words to remember

Look at the words below and say them out
loud a few times. Conceal the Italian with
the cover flap and try to remember each one
in turn. Practice the words on the right also.

lo zucchero
loh tsookkeroh
sugar

il caffè macchiato eel kaffay makeeatoh	*espresso with a little milk*
la tisana lah teezanah	*herbal tea*
il tè con latte eel tay kon lattay	*tea with milk*
il panino eel paneenoh	*sandwich*

il caffè (espresso)
eel kaffay (espressoh)
small, black coffee

Cultural tip Italians are not big tea-drinkers and
when they do have tea, they add some lemon rather than
milk. So if you want milk in your tea, you may have to ask
for a little cold milk ("un po' di latte freddo").

In conversation

**Vorrei un cappuccino,
per favore.**
vorray oon
kappoocheenoh, per
favoray

*I'd like a cappuccino,
please.*

Altro, signore?
altroh, seennyoray

Anything else, sir?

Ha delle brioche?
ah dellay breeosh

*Do you have any
croissants?*

4 Useful phrases

Learn these phrases. Read the English under the pictures and say the phrase in Italian as shown on the right. Then cover up the answers on the right and test yourself.

la brioche
lah breeosh
croissant

la crema
lah kremah
custard cream

il cappuccino
eel kappoocheenoh
coffee with frothy milk

Some coffee, please.

Un caffè, per favore.
oon kaffay, per favoray

Anything else?

Altro?
altroh

A croissant, too, please.

Anche una brioche, per favore.
ankay oonah breeosh, per favoray

How much is that?

Quant'è?
kwantay

Sì, certo.
see, chertoh

Yes, certainly.

Allora, prendo una brioche. Quant'è?
allorah, prendoh oonah breeosh. kwantay

I'll have a croissant, then. How much is that?

Quattro euro, per favore.
kwattroh ayooroh, per favoray

Four euros, please.

1 Warm up

Say "I'd like."
(pp.18–19)

Say "I don't have a
brother." (pp.14–15)

Ask "Do you have any
croissants?"
(pp.18–19)

Al ristorante
In the restaurant

There are a variety of eating places
in Italy. In a bar you can find a few
snacks. A **trattoria** is a traditional
restaurant with fast service. In more
formal restaurants, it is often necessary
to make reservations. Pizzerias are a
relaxed and cheap way of dining out,
and are ideal for big groups.

2 Words to remember

Memorize these words. Conceal the Italian
with the cover flap and test yourself.

cup **7**

il menù *eel menoo*	*menu*
la lista dei vini *lah leesta day veenee*	*wine list*
i primi piatti *ee preemee peeattee*	*appetizers*
i secondi piatti *ee seekondee peeattee*	*main courses*
i dessert *ee dessert*	*desserts*
la colazione *lah kolatseeonay*	*breakfast*
il pranzo *eel pranzoh*	*lunch*
la cena *lah chenah*	*dinner*

knife **6**

5 *spoon* **4** *fork*

3 In conversation

**Buongiorno, ha un
tavolo per quattro?**
*bwonjornoh, ah oon
tavoloh per kwattroh*

*Hello. Do you have a
table for four?*

Ha la prenotazione?
ah lah prenotatseeonay

*Do you have a
reservation?*

Sì, a nome Gatti.
see, anomay gattee

*Yes, in the name of
Gatti.*

4 Match and repeat

Look at the numbered items in this table setting and match them with the Italian words on the right. Read the Italian words aloud. Now, conceal the Italian with the cover flap and test yourself.

glass **1**

8 saucer

1 **il bicchiere**
   eel beekkyayray

2 **il tovagliolo**
   eel tovallyohloh

3 **il piatto**
   eel peeattoh

4 **la forchetta**
   lah forkettah

5 **il cucchiaio**
   eel kookee-ayoh

6 **il coltello**
   eel koltelloh

7 **la tazza**
   lah tattsah

8 **il piattino**
   eel peeahteenoh

5 Useful phrases

Practice these phrases and then test yourself using the cover flap to conceal the Italian.

napkin **2**

What do you have for dessert?	**Cosa avete come dessert?** kozah avaytay komay dessert
The check, please.	**Il conto, per favore.** eel kontoh, per favoray

plate **3**

Fumatori o non fumatori?
foomatoree oh non fumatoree

Smoking or nonsmoking?

Non fumatori, per favore.
non foomatoree, per favoray

Nonsmoking, please.

Certo. Ecco.
chertoh. ekkoh

Fine. Here you are.

Volere
To want

In this section, you will learn the different forms of a verb that are essential to everyday conversation, **volere** (*to want*), including a useful polite form, **vorrei** (*I would like*). Remember to use this form when requesting something because **voglio** (*I want*) may sound too strong.

2 Volere: to want

Say the different forms of **volere** (*to want*) aloud. Use the cover flap to test yourself and, when you are confident, practice the sample sentences below.

(io) voglio vollyoh	*I want*
(tu) vuoi vwoee	*you want* *(informal singular)*
(Lei) vuole vwolay	*you want* *(formal singular)*
(lui/lei) vuole vwolay	*he/she wants*
(noi) vogliamo vollyamoh	*we want*
(voi) volete voletay	*you want* *(plural)*
(loro) vogliono vollyonoh	*they want*
Lei vuole un'auto nuova. lay vwolay oon a-ootoh nwovah	*She wants a new car.*
Vogliamo andare in vacanza. vollyamoh andaray een vakantsah	*We want to go on vacation.*

Voglio delle caramelle.
vollyoh dellay karamayllay
I want some candy.

█ Conversational tip In Italian "del" the word for "some" changes depending on what follows. For example, "Voglio del caffè" (I want some coffee, masculine singular), "Voglio della birra" (I want some beer, feminine singular), "Voglio dei limoni" (I want some lemons, masculine plural), and "Voglio delle caramelle" (I want some sweets, feminine plural). "Della" may be shortened to "dell'" before a vowel.

3 Polite requests

There is a form of **volere** used for polite requests: **(io) vorrei** (*I would like*), as in **Vorrei un caffè** (*I'd like a coffee*). Practice the following sample sentences and then test yourself using the cover flap.

I'd like a beer.
Vorrei una birra.
vorray oonah beerah

I'd like a table for tonight.
Vorrei un tavolo per stasera.
vorray oon tavoloh per staserah

I'd like the menu, please.
Vorrei il menù, per favore.
vorray eel menoo, per favoray

4 Put into practice

Join in this conversation. Read the Italian beside the pictures on the left and then follow the instructions to make your reply in Italian. Test yourself by hiding the answers with the cover flap.

Buonasera. Ha la prenotazione?
bwonasayrah. ah lah prenotatseeonay
Good evening. Do you have a reservation?

Say: No, but I would like a table for three.

No, ma vorrei un tavolo per tre.
noh, mah vorray oon tavoloh per tray

Benissimo. Che tavolo vuole?
beneesseemoh. kay tavoloh vwolay
Fine. Which table would you like?

Say: Near the window, please.

Vicino alla finestra, per favore.
veecheenoh allah feenestrah, per favoray

Le pietanze
Dishes

Italy is famous for its cuisine and the quality of its restaurants. It also offers a wide variety of regional dishes. Pasta is a typical Italian dish, prepared in dozens of different ways. Although traditional Italian cuisine is meat-based, many restaurants now offer a vegetarian menu.

Cultural tip In many restaurants you will be able to choose a cheaper set menu "il menù fisso" or "il menù turistico." Salad ("l'insalata") is generally served as a side dish ("il contorno").

Match and repeat

Look at the numbered items and match them to the Italian words in the panel on the left.

1 **la verdura**
lah vairdoorah

2 **la frutta**
lah froottah

3 **il formaggio**
eel formajjoh

4 **la frutta secca**
la froottah sekkah

5 **la minestra**
lah meenestrah

6 **il pollo**
eel polloh

7 **il pesce**
eel peshay

8 **la pasta**
lah pastah

9 **i frutti di mare**
ee froottee dee maray

10 **la carne**
lah karnay

❶ *vegetables*

❷ *fruit*

❸ *cheese*

❺ *soup*

❻ *chicken*

❽ *pasta*

❾ *seafood*

3 Words to remember: cooking methods

The ending may vary depending on the gender of item described.

fried (m/f)	**fritto/a** freettoh/ah
grilled	**alla griglia** allah greellyah
roasted (m/f)	**arrosto** arrostoh
boiled (m/f)	**lesso/a** layssoh/ah
steamed	**al vapore** al vaporay
rare (meat)	**al sangue** al sangway

**Vorrei una bistecca
ben cotta.**
vorray oona beestekkah
ben kottah
*I'd like my steak
well done.*

6 Say it

What is "al vapore"?

I'm allergic to
seafood.

I'd like a beer.

4 Words to remember: drinks

Familiarize yourself with these words.

water	**l'acqua** *(f)* lahkkwah
sparkling water	**l'acqua gassata** *(f)* lahkkwah gassatah
still water	**l'acqua naturale** *(f)* lahkkwah natooralay
wine	**il vino** eel veenoh
beer	**la birra** lah beerah
fruit juice	**il succo di frutta** eel sookkoh dee froottah

❹ *nuts*

5 Useful phrases

Practice these phrases and then test yourself.

I am a vegetarian.	**Sono vegetariano/a.** sonoh vejetareeanoh/ah
I am allergic to nuts.	**Sono allergico/a alla frutta secca.** sonoh allerjeekoh/ah allah froottah sekkah
What are "tagliatelle"?	**Cosa sono le tagliatelle?** kozah sonoh lay tallyatellay

❼ *fish*

❿ *meat*

Risposte
Answers
Cover with flap

Ripassa e ripeti
Review and repeat

1 What food?

1 **lo zucchero**
loh tsookkeroh

2 **la verdura**
lah vairdoorah

3 **i frutti di mare**
ee froottee dee
maray

4 **la carne**
lah karnay

5 **il bicchiere**
eel beekkyayray

1 What food?

Name the numbered items.

1 sugar

2 vegetables

3 seafood

4 meat

glass **5**

2 This is my...

1 **Questo è mio marito.**
kwestoh ay meeoh mareetoh

2 **Questa è mia figlia.**
kwestah ay meeah feellyah

3 **Queste sono le mie sorelle.**
kwestay sonoh lay meeay sorellay

2 This is my...

Say these phrases in Italian.
Use "mio," "mia," "miei," or "mie."

1 *This is my husband.*

2 *This is my daughter.*

3 *These are my sisters.*

3 I'd like...

1 **Vorrei un caffè.**
vorray oon caffay

2 **Vorrei un cappuccino.**
vorray oon kappoocheenoh

3 **Vorrei una brioche.**
vorray oonah breeosh

4 **Vorrei lo zucchero.**
vorray loh tsookkeroh

3 I'd like...

Say "I'd like" the following:

4 sugar

croissant **3**

cappuccino **2**

1 black coffee

Risposte
Answers
Cover with flap

6 *pasta*

knife 7

8 *cheese*

beer 10

9 *napkin*

What food?

6 **la pasta**
lah pastah

7 **il coltello**
eel koltelloh

8 **il formaggio**
eel formajjoh

9 **il tovagliolo**
eel tovallyohloh

10 **la birra**
lah beerrah

Restaurant

You arrive at a restaurant. Join in the conversation, replying in Italian where you see the English prompts.

Buonasera.
1 *Ask "Do you have a table for one?"*

Fumatori o non fumatori?
2 *Say "Nonsmoking."*

Sì. Ecco.
3 *Say "I'd like the menu, please."*

Vuole anche la lista dei vini?
4 *Say "No. Sparkling water, please."*

Ecco.
5 *Say "I don't have a glass."*

Restaurant

1 **Ha un tavolo per uno?**
ah oon tavoloh per oonoh

2 **Non fumatori.**
non foomatoree

3 **Vorrei il menù, per favore.**
vorray eel menoo, per favoray

4 **No, acqua gassata, per favore.**
noh, ahkkwah gassatah, per favoray

5 **Non ho il bicchiere.**
non oh eel beekkyeray

1 Warm up

How do you say "he is" and "they are"? (pp.14–15)

Now say "he is not" and "they are not." (pp.14–15)

What is Italian for "my mother"? (pp.10–11)

I giorni e i mesi
Days and months

In Italian, days of the week (**i giorni della settimana**) and months (**i mesi**) do not have capital letters. Notice that with months you generally use **in**: **in ottobre** (*in October*); with days you use nothing: **lunedì** (*on Monday*), but when it means every Monday you use the article (**il/la**): **il lunedì** (*on Mondays*).

2 Words to remember: days of the week

Familiarize yourself with these words and test yourself using the flap.

lunedì loonedee	*Monday*
martedì martedee	*Tuesday*
mercoledì merkoledee	*Wednesday*
giovedì jovedee	*Thursday*
venerdì venerdee	*Friday*
sabato sabatoh	*Saturday*
domenica domeneekah	*Sunday*
oggi ojjee	*today*
domani domanee	*tomorrow*
ieri yayree	*yesterday*

Ci vediamo domani.
chee vedeeamoh domanee
We meet tomorrow.

Ho una prenotazione per oggi.
oh oonah prenota-tseeonay per ojjee
I have a reservation for today.

3 Useful phrases: days

Learn these phrases and then test yourself using the cover flap.

La riunione non è martedì. lah reeooneeonay non ay martedee	*The meeting isn't on Tuesday.*
La domenica lavoro. lah domeneekah lavoroh	*I work on Sundays.*

4 Words to remember: months of the year

Familiarize yourself with these words and test yourself using the flap.

January	**gennaio** jennaheeoh
February	**febbraio** febbraheeoh
March	**marzo** martsoh
April	**aprile** apreelay
May	**maggio** majjeeoh
June	**giugno** jooneeoh
July	**luglio** loollyoh
August	**agosto** agostoh
September	**settembre** settembray
October	**ottobre** ottobray
November	**novembre** novembray
December	**dicembre** deechembray
month	**mese** mezay
year	**anno** annoh

**Il nostro anniversario
è in luglio.**
eel nostroh anneever-
sareeoh ay een loollyoh
*Our anniversary is
in July.*

Natale è in dicembre.
natalay ay een
deechembray
*Christmas is in
December.*

5 Useful phrases: months

Learn these phrases and then test yourself using the cover flap.

My children are on vacation in August.	**I miei bambini sono in vacanza in agosto.** ee mee-ayee bambeenee sonoh een vakantsah een agostoh
My birthday is in June.	**Il mio compleanno è in giugno.** eel mee-oh kompleahnnoh ay een jooneeoh

1 Warm up

Count in Italian from 1 to 10. (pp.10–11)

Say "I have a reservation." (pp.20–1)

Say "The meeting is on Wednesday." (pp.28–9)

L'ora e i numeri
Time and numbers

On a day-to-day basis Italians use the 12-hour clock, sometimes adding **di mattina** (*in the morning*), **di pomeriggio** (*in the afternoon*), **di sera** (*in the evening*), or **di notte** (*at night*). To say the time you say **Sono le...**, as in **Sono le dieci** (*It's ten o'clock*), except for *It's one o'clock*, which is **È l'una**.

2 Words to remember: time

Memorize how to tell the time in Italian.

l'una loonah	*one o'clock*
l'una e cinque loonah ay cheenkway	*five after one*
l'una e un quarto loonah ay oon kwartoh	*quarter after one*
l'una e mezzo loonah ay metsoh	*one-thirty*
l'una e venti loonah ay ventee	*one-twenty*
le due meno un quarto lay dooay menoh oon kwartoh	*quarter to two*
le due meno dieci lay dooay meno deeaychee	*ten to two*

3 Useful phrases

Learn these phrases and then test yourself using the cover flap.

Che ore sono? kay oray sonoh	*What time is it?*
A che ora vuole la colazione? ah kay orah voo-olay lah kolatseeonay	*What time do you want breakfast?*
Ho una prenotazione per le dodici. oh oonah prenotatseeonay per lay dodeechee	*I have a reservation for twelve o'clock.*

4 Words to remember: higher numbers

To say 21, 31, and so on, you say **ventuno**, **trentuno**, etc. After that, just add the number as in **ventidue** (22), **ventitré** (23), **trentadue** (32), **trentatré** (33).

To say the date, you generally use the regular number: **Oggi è il 26 settembre** (*Today is September 26th*).

The exception is the first day of the month when you say "the first," as in **Domani è il primo febbraio** (*Tomorrow is the first of February*).

eleven	**undici** oondeechee
twelve	**dodici** dodeechee
thirteen	**tredici** traydeechee
fourteen	**quattordici** kwattordeechee
fifteen	**quindici** kweendeechee
sixteen	**sedici** sedeechee
seventeen	**diciassette** deechassettay
eighteen	**diciotto** deechottoh
nineteen	**diciannove** deechannovay
twenty	**venti** ventee
thirty	**trenta** trentah
forty	**quaranta** kwarantah
fifty	**cinquanta** cheenkwantah
sixty	**sessanta** sessantah
seventy	**settanta** settantah
eighty	**ottanta** ottantah
ninety	**novanta** novantah
hundred	**cento** chentoh
three hundred	**trecento** traychentoh
thousand	**mille** meellay
ten thousand	**diecimila** deeaycheemeelah
two hundred thousand	**duecentomila** dooaychentomeelah
one million	**un milione** oon meeleeonay

Sono ottantacinque euro.
sonoh ottantacheenkway ayooroh
That's eighty-five euros.

5 Say it

twenty-five

sixty-eight

eighty-four

ninety-one

It's five to ten.

It's eleven-thirty.

What time is lunch?

Gli appuntamenti
Appointments

1

Say the days of the week. (pp.28–9)

Say "It's three o'clock." (pp.30–1)

What's the Italian for "today," "tomorrow," and "yesterday"? (pp.28–9)

Business in Italy is still generally conducted more formally than in the United States; always address business contacts as **Lei**. Italians also tend to take a longer lunch break and, except in big cities, people often go home for their noon meal.

2 Useful phrases

Learn these phrases and then test yourself.

Fissiamo un appuntamento per domani? feesseeamoh oon appoontamentoh per domanee	*Shall we meet tomorrow?*
Con chi? kon kee	*With whom?*
Quando è libero/a? kwandoh ay leeberoh/ah	*When are you free?*
Mi dispiace, sono impegnato/a. mee deespeeachay, sonoh eempennyatoh/ah	*I'm sorry, I'm busy.*
Va bene giovedì? vah benay jovedee	*How about Thursday?*
Per me va bene. per may vah benay	*That's good for me.*

la stretta di mano
lah strettah dee manoh
handshake

Benvenuto.
benvenootoh
Welcome.

3 In conversation

Buongiorno. Ho un appuntamento.
bwonjornoh. oh oon appoontamentoh

Hello. I have an appointment.

Con chi?
kon kee

With whom?

Con il signor Baroni.
kon eel seennyor baronee

With Mr. Baroni.

4 Put into practice

Practice these phrases. Then cover up the text on the right and say the answering part of the dialogue in Italian. Check your answers and repeat if necessary.

Fissiamo un appuntamento per giovedì?
feesseeamoh oon appoontamentoh per jovedee
Shall we meet on Thursday?

Say: Sorry, I'm busy.

Mi dispiace, giovedì sono impegnato.
mee deespeeachay, jovedee sonoh eempennyatoh

Quando è libero?
kwandoh ay liberoh
When are you free?

Say: Tuesday afternoon.

Martedì pomeriggio.
martedee pomereejjoh

Per me va bene.
per may vah benay
That's good for me.

Ask: What time?

A che ora?
ah kay orah

Alle quattro, se per Lei va bene.
allay kwattroh, say per lay vah benay
At four o'clock, if that's good for you.

Say: It's good for me.

Per me va bene.
per may vah benay

Benissimo, a che ora?
beneesseemoh, ah kay orah

OK, at what time?

Alle tre, ma sono un po' in ritardo.
allay tray, mah sonoh oon poh een reetardoh

At three o'clock, but I'm a little late.

Non si preoccupi. Prego, si accomodi.
non see prayokkoopee. pregoh, see akkomodee

Don't worry. Take a seat, please.

1 Warm up

How do you say "I'm sorry"? (pp.32–3)

Say "I'd like an appointment." (pp.32–3)

How do you say "with whom?" in Italian? (pp.32–3)

Al telefono
On the telephone

In Italy you always dial the full area code (**il prefisso**) and the number. You can call from a public phone (**il telefono pubblico**) using a phone card. Italy's general emergency number is 113; or you can call the Carabinieri on 112; ambulance (**l'ambulanza**), 118; fire department (**i vigili del fuoco**), 115.

2 Match and repeat

Match the numbered items to the Italian in the panel on the left and test yourself.

1 **il caricabatterie**
  eel karikabatereeay

charger ❶

2 **la segreteria telefonica**
  la segretereeah telayfoneekah

3 **il telefono**
  eel telayfonoh

4 **il cellulare**
  eel chelloolaray

5 **la scheda telefonica**
  la skaydah telefoneekah

6 **gli auricolari**
  lly awreekolaree

❸ *telephone*

cell phone ❹

❻ *headphones*   *phone card* ❺

3 In conversation

Pronto? Bonanni.
prontoh? bonannee

Hello? Bonanni's.

Buongiorno. Vorrei parlare con il dottor Pieri.
bwonjornoh. vorray parlaray kon eel dottor pyayree

Hello. I'd like to speak to Dr. Pieri.

Chi parla?
kee parlah

Who's speaking?

4 Useful phrases

Practice these phrases. Then test yourself using the cover flap.

I'd like an outside line.

Vorrei una linea esterna.
vorray oonah leeneah esternah

Vorrei fare una telefonata a carico.
vorray faray oonah telefonatah ah kareekoh
I'd like to make a collect call.

I'd like to speak to Federico Martini.

Vorrei parlare con Federico Martini.
vorray parlaray kon fedayreekoh marteenee

2 answering machine

Can I leave a message?

Posso lasciare un messaggio?
possoh lasharay oon messajjoh

5 Say it

I'd like to speak to Mr. Hachart.

Can I leave a message for Emma?

Sorry, I have the wrong number.

Scusi, ho sbagliato numero.
skoozee, oh sballyatoh noomayroh

Luciano Salvetti, della tipografia Bartoli.
loochanoh salvettee, della teepografeeah bartolee

Luciano Salvetti of Bartoli Printers.

Mi dispiace, la linea è occupata.
mee deespeeachay, lah leeneah ay okkoopatah

I'm sorry. The line is busy.

Può farmi richiamare, per favore?
puoh farmee reekeeamaray, per favoray

Can he call me back, please?

Ripassa e ripeti
Review and repeat

1 Sums

1 **sedici**
sedeechee

2 **trentanove**
trentanovay

3 **cinquantatré**
cheenkwantatray

4 **settantaquattro**
settantakwattroh

5 **novantanove**
novantanovay

6 **quarantuno**
kwarantoonoh

2 To want

1 **vuole**
vwolay

2 **vogliamo**
vollyamoh

3 **vogliono**
vollyonoh

4 **vuoi**
vwoee

5 **voglio**
vollyoh

6 **volete**
voletay

1 Sums

Say the answers to these sums out loud in Italian. Then check to see if you remembered correctly.

1 $10 + 6 = ?$

2 $14 + 25 = ?$

3 $66 - 13 = ?$

4 $40 + 34 = ?$

5 $90 + 9 = ?$

6 $46 - 5 = ?$

3 Telephones

What are the numbered items in Italian?

cell phone ❶

phone card ❸

2 To want

Fill in the blanks with the right form of **volere** (*to want*).

1 **Signora, _____ un caffè?**

2 **Io e Matteo _____ un tavolo per due.**

3 (loro) _____ delle caramelle.

4 (tu) _____ una birra?

5 (io) _____ una macchina nuova.

6 (voi) _____ dei bicchieri?

answering machine **2**

telephone **4**   *headphones* **5**

3 Telephones

1 **il cellulare**
eel chelloolaray

2 **la segreteria telefonica**
la segretereeah telayfoneekah

3 **la scheda telefonica**
la skaydah telayfoneekah

4 **il telefono**
eel telayfonoh

5 **gli auricolari**
lly awreekolaree

4 When?

What do these sentences mean?

1 **La riunione è giovedì.**

2 **Voglio andare in vacanza domani.**

3 **Il mio compleanno è in agosto.**

4 **Il nostro anniversario è in dicembre.**

4 When?

1 *The meeting is on Thursday.*

2 *I want to go on vacation tomorrow.*

3 *My birthday is in August.*

4 *Our anniversary is in December.*

5 Time

Say these times in Italian.

5 Time

1 **l'una**
loonah

2 **l'una e cinque**
loonah ay cheenkway

3 **l'una e venti**
loonah ay ventee

4 **l'una e mezzo**
loonah ay metsoh

5 **l'una e un quarto**
loonah ay oon kwartoh

6 **le due meno dieci**
lay dooay menoh deeaychee

Count to 100 in tens.
(pp.10–11 and
pp.30–1)

Ask "at what time?"
(pp.30–1)

Say "half-past one."
(pp.30–1)

Alla biglietteria
At the ticket office

In Italy you must be sure to validate
(**convalidare**) your ticket before getting
on the train by stamping it in one of
the special small yellow machines
installed in every train station for this
purpose. Fines are imposed on
travelers who have forgotten to
validate their tickets.

2 Words to remember

Learn these words and then test yourself.

la stazione lah statseeonay	*station*
il treno eel trenoh	*train*
la prenotazione la prenotatseeonay	*reservation*
il biglietto eel beellyettoh	*ticket*
sola andata solah andatah	*one-way*
andata e ritorno andatah ay reetornoh	*round-trip*
prima/seconda classe preemah/sekondah klassay	*first/second class*
la coincidenza la koeencheedentsa	*connection*

il passeggero
eel passejjayroh
passenger

il cartello
eel kartelloh
sign

La stazione è affollata.
lah statseeonay ay
affollahtah
The station is crowded.

3 In conversation

**Due biglietti per
Roma, per favore.**
dooay beellyettee per
rohmah, per favoray

*Two tickets to Rome,
please.*

Andata e ritorno?
andatah ay reetornoh

Return?

**Sì. C'è la prenotazione
obbligatoria?**
see. chay lah
prenotatseeonay
obbleegatoryah

*Yes. Do I need to
reserve seats?*

4 Useful phrases

Learn these phrases and then test yourself using the cover flap.

How much is a ticket to Genoa?	**Quanto costa un biglietto per Genova?** kwantoh kostah oon beellyettoh per jenovah
Do you accept credit cards?	**Accettate la carta di credito?** acchettatay lah kartah dee kredeetoh
Do I have to change trains?	**Devo cambiare?** devoh kambeearay
Which platform does the train leave from?	**Da quale binario parte il treno?** dah kwalay beenareeoh partay eel trenoh
Are there discounts?	**Ci sono delle riduzioni?** chee sonoh dellay reedootseeonee
What time does the train to Naples leave?	**A che ora parte il treno per Napoli?** ah kay orah partay eel trenoh per napolee

Il treno per Firenze è in ritardo.
eel trenoh per firentsay ay een reetardoh
The train to Florence is late.

il binario
eel beenareeoh
platform

5 Say it

Which platform does the train to Genoa leave from?

Three return tickets to Naples, please.

🇮🇹 **Cultural tip** Most train stations now have automatic ticket machines ("la biglietteria automatica") that accept credit and debit cards as well as cash.

No. Sono quaranta euro.
noh. sonoh kwarantah ayooroh

No. It's forty euros.

Accettate la carta di credito?
acchettatay lah kartah dee kredeetoh

Do you take credit cards?

Certo. Il treno parte dal binario uno.
chertoh. eel trenoh partay dal beenareeoh oonoh

Certainly. The train leaves from platform one.

1 Warm up

How do you say "train"? (pp.38–9)

What does "Da quale binario parte il treno?" mean? (pp.38–9)

Ask "When are you free?" (pp.32–3)

Andare e prendere
To go and to take

Andare (*to go*) and **prendere** (*to take*) are essential verbs in Italian that you will need to use frequently in everyday conversation as you find your way around. You can also use **prendere** when you talk about food and drink—for example, to say **prendo un caffè** (*I'll have coffee*).

2 Andare: to go

Say the different forms of **andare** (*to go*) aloud. Use the cover flaps to test yourself and, when you are confident, practice the sample sentences below.

(io) vado (eeoh) vadoh	*I go*
(tu) vai (too) vaee	*you go (informal singular)*
(Lei) va (lay) vah	*you go (formal singular)*
(lui/lei) va (looee/lay) vah	*he/she/it goes*
(noi) andiamo (noy) andeeamoh	*we go*
(voi) andate (voy) andatay	*you go (plural)*
(loro) vanno (loroh) vannoh	*they go*
Dove va, signora? dovay vah, seennyorah	*Where are you going, madam?*
Vorrei andare in treno. vorray andaray een trenoh	*I'd like to go by train.*

Vado a Pisa.
vadoh ah peesah
I am going to Pisa.

Conversational tip In Italian the present tense includes a sense of continuous action. You use the same verb form to say "I go" and "I am going." "Vado a Roma" means both "I am going to Rome" and "I go to Rome." The same is true of other verbs; for example, "prendo il taxi" means "I am taking the taxi" and "I take the taxi."

3 Prendere: to take

Say the different forms of **prendere** (*to take*) aloud and test yourself.

I take	**(io) prendo** (eeoh) prendoh
you take (informal)	**(tu) prendi** (too) prendee
you take (formal)	**(Lei) prende** (lay) prenday
he/she/it takes	**(lui/lei) prende** (looee/lay) prenday
we take	**(noi) prendiamo** (noy) prendeeamoh
you take (plural)	**(voi) prendete** (voy) prendetay
they take	**(loro) prendono** (loroh) prendonoh

Prendo la metro tutti i giorni.
prendoh lah metroh tottee ee jornee
I take the metro every day.

I don't want to take a taxi.	**Non voglio prendere un taxi.** non vollyoh prenderay oon taxee

Take the first left.	**Prenda la prima a sinistra.** prenda lah preemah ah seeneestrah

He'll have the veal.	**Lui prende il vitello.** looee prenday eel veetelloh

4 Put into practice

Cover the text on the right and complete the dialogue in Italian.

	Dove va? dovay vah *Where are you going?*	**Vado alla stazione.** vadoh allah statseeonay
	Say: I'm going to the station.	

Vuole prendere la metro? vwolay prenderay lah metroh *Do you want to take the metro?*	**No, voglio andare in autobus.** noh, vollyoh andaray een a-ootoboos
Say: No, I want to go by bus.	

1 Warm up

Say "I'd like to go to the station." (pp.40–1)

Ask "Where are you going?" (pp.40–1)

Say "fruit" and "cheese." (pp.24–5)

Taxi, autobus e metro
Taxi, bus, and metro

In Italy you generally don't hail taxis, but go to a taxi stand. You can buy bus tickets at a newsstand and then validate them in the machine on the bus. You can use the same tickets both on the buses and on the metro.

2 Words to remember

Familiarize yourself with these words.

l'autobus *(m)* la-ootoboos	*bus (local)*
il pullman eel poolman	*bus (long-distance)*
la stazione dei pullman/della metro lah statseeonay day poolman/dellah metroh	*bus/metro station*
la fermata dell'autobus lah fermatah della-ootoboos	*bus stop*
il biglietto eel beellyettoh	*fare*
il posteggio dei taxi eel postejjoh day taxee	*taxi stand*

Passa di qui il quarantasei?
passah dee kwee eel kwarantasay
Does the Route 46 bus stop here?

3 In conversation: taxi

Al mercato di San Lorenzo, per favore.
al merkatoh dee san lorentsoh, per favoray

To the San Lorenzo market, please.

Benissimo, signore.
beneesseemoh, seennyoray

Very well, sir.

Mi lasci qui, per favore.
mee lashee kwee, per favoray

Can you drop me here, please?

4 Useful phrases

Learn these phrases and then test yourself using the cover flap.

I'd like a taxi to go to the Colosseum.

Vorrei un taxi per andare al Colosseo.
vorray oon taxee per andaray al kolossayoh

When is the next bus to the Capitol?

Quando passa il prossimo autobus per il Campidoglio?
kwandoh passah eel prosseemoh a-ootoboos per eel kampeedollyoh

How do you get to the Vatican?

Scusi, per andare al Vaticano?
skoozee, per andaray al vateekahnoh

Please wait for me.

Mi aspetti, per favore.
mee aspettee, per favoray

Cultural tip In Italy the metro exists only in Milan and Rome. There are only a few lines and they are identified by numbers (M1, M2, M3 in Milan) or letters of the alphabet (MA, MB in Rome). Look for the relevant end station to find the direction you need.

6 Say it

Do you go to the train station?

The Vatican, please.

When's the next coach to Rome?

5 In conversation: bus

Scusi, va al museo?
skoozee, vah al moozayoh

Do you go to the museum?

Sì. Non è lontano.
see. non ay lontanoh

Yes. It's not very far.

Può dirmi quando devo scendere?
pwoh deermee kwandoh devoh shenderay

Can you tell me when to get off?

1 Warm up

How do you say "I have..."? (pp.14–15)

Say "my father," "my sister," and "my parents." (pp.12–13)

Say "I'm going to Rome." (pp.40–1)

In auto
On the road

Be sure to familiarize yourself with the Italian rules of the road before driving in Italy. Italian **autostrade** (*expressways*) are fast but expensive toll (**il pedaggio**) roads. You usually take a ticket as you enter the expressway and pay according to the distance traveled as you leave it.

2 Match and repeat

Match the numbered items to the list on the left, then test yourself.

1 **il bagagliaio**
eel bagallyaeeoh

2 **il parabrezza**
eel parabretsah

3 **il cofano**
eel kofanoh

4 **la ruota**
lah rwotah

5 **la gomma**
lah gommah

6 **lo sportello**
loh sportelloh

7 **il paraurti**
eel parahoortee

8 **i fari**
ee faree

> 🇮🇹 **Cultural tip** In Italy many gas stations still have a pump attendant, and many are closed for lunch. Sometimes you can serve yourself and pay a cheaper rate.

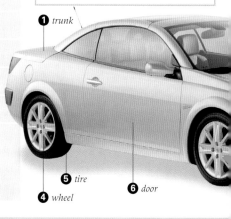

❶ *trunk*

❺ *tire*

❻ *door*

❹ *wheel*

3 Road signs

Senso unico
senso uneekoh

One way

Rotatoria
rotatoreeah

Roundabout

Dare la precedenza
daray lah prechedentsah

Yield

4 Useful phrases

Learn these phrases and then test yourself using the cover flap.

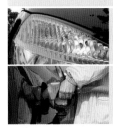

My turn signal doesn't work.	**La freccia non funziona.** lah frechah non foontseeonah
Fill it up, please.	**Il pieno, per favore.** eel pyaynoh, per favoray

5 Words to remember

Familiarize yourself with these words, then test yourself using the flap.

6 Say it

My gearbox doesn't work.

I have a flat tire.

driver's license	**la patente** lah patentay
gasoline	**la benzina** lah bendseenah
diesel	**il gasolio** gazolyoh
oil	**l'olio** *(m)* lohlyoh
engine	**il motore** eel motoray
gearbox	**il cambio** eel kambeeoh
turn signal	**la freccia** lah frechah
exhaust	**la marmitta** lah marmeettah
flat tire	**la gomma a terra** lah gommah ah terrah

❷ *windshield*

❸ *hood*

MEGANE

headlights ❽

❼ *bumper*

Diritto di precedenza
deereettoh dee prechedentsah

Priority road

Divieto di accesso
deevyaytoh dee acchessoh

Do not enter

Sosta vietata
sostah veeaytatah

No parking

Risposte
Answers
Cover with flap

Ripassa e ripeti
Review and repeat

1 Transportation

1 **l'autobus**
la-ootoboos

2 **il taxi**
eel taxee

3 **l'auto**
la-ootoh

4 **la bicicletta**
lah beecheeklettah

5 **la metro**
lah metroh

1 Transportation

Name these forms of transportation in Italian.

bus **1**

taxi **2**

2 Go and take

1 **va**
vah

2 **prendiamo**
prendeeamoh

3 **vado**
vadoh

4 **prende**
prenday

5 **vanno**
vannoh

6 **prendi**
prendee

2 Go and take

Use the correct form of the verb in brackets to fill in the blanks.

1 Dove _____ l'autobus? (andare)

2 (noi) _____ un taxi. (prendere)

3 (io) _____ a Pisa. (andare)

4 _____ un caffè, signor Gatti? (prendere)

5 (loro) _____ in treno. (andare)

6 (tu) _____ la seconda a sinistra. (prendere)

3 car

4 bicycle

metro **5**

3 Lei or tu?

Use the correct form of you.

1 *You are in a café. Ask "Do you have croissants?"*

2 *You are with a friend. Ask "Do you want a beer?"*

3 *You are talking to a business contact. Ask "Do you have an appointment?"*

4 *You are on the bus. Ask "Do you go to the station?"*

5 *Ask your friend where she's going tomorrow.*

6 *Ask your (female) client "Are you free on Wednesday?"*

3 Lei or tu?

1 **Ha delle brioche?**
ah dellay breeosh

2 **Vuoi una birra?**
vwoee oonah beerah

3 **Ha un appuntamento?**
ah oon appoontamentoh

4 **Va alla stazione?**
vah allah statseeonay

5 **Dove vai domani?**
dovay vaee domanee

6 **È libera mercoledì?**
ay leeberah merkoledee

4 Tickets

You're buying tickets at a train station. Join in the conversation, replying in Italian following the numbered English prompts.

Buongiorno.
1 *I'd like two tickets to Ferrara.*

Solo andata o andata e ritorno?
2 *Round-trip, please.*

Sono trenta euro.
3 *What time does the train leave?*

Alle quindici e dieci.
4 *What platform does the train leave from?*

Dal binario sette.
5 *Thank you.*

4 Tickets

1 **Vorrei due biglietti per Ferrara.**
vorray dooay beellyettee per ferrarah

2 **Andata e ritorno, per favore.**
andatah ay reetornoh, per favoray

3 **A che ora parte il treno?**
ah kay orah partay eel trenoh

4 **Da quale binario parte il treno?**
dah kwalay beenareeoh partay eel trenoh

5 **Grazie.**
gratseeay

1 Warm up

Ask "How do you get to the museum?" (pp.42–3)

Say "I want to take the metro" and "I don't want to take a taxi." (pp.40–1)

In città
Around town

Most Italian towns (**la città**) and larger villages (**il paese**) still have a market day for fresh produce and a thriving local community of small shops and businesses. There may be parking restrictions in the downtown area. In Rome, parking in the central **zona tutelata** is prohibited on weekdays.

2 Match and repeat

Match the numbered locations to the words in the panel.

1 **il municipio**
eel moonee-cheepeeoh

2 **la chiesa**
lah keeayzah

3 **il ponte**
eel pontay

4 **il centro città**
eel chentroh cheettah

5 **il parcheggio**
eel parkejjoh

6 **la piazza**
lah peeatsah

7 **il museo**
eel moozayoh

church ❷

❶ *town hall*

❸ *bridge*

downtown ❹

3 Words to remember

Familiarize yourself with these words and test yourself using the cover flap.

il benzinaio eel bentseenaeeoh	*gas station*
l'azienda turistica *(f)* latsyayndah tooreesteekah	*tourist information*
la piscina lah peesheenah	*swimming pool*
la biblioteca lah beebleeotaykah	*library*

❻ *square*

4 Useful phrases

Learn these phrases and then test yourself using the cover flap.

Is there an art gallery in town?	**C'è una pinacoteca in città?** chay oonah peenacotekah een cheettah
Is it far from here?	**È lontano da qui?** ay lontanoh da kwee
There is a swimming pool near the bridge.	**C'è una piscina vicino al ponte.** chay oonah peesheenah veecheenoh al pontay
There isn't a library.	**Non c'è una biblioteca.** non chay oonah beebleeotaykah

Il duomo è in centro.
eel dwomoh ay een chentroh
The cathedral is downtown.

5 Put into practice

Join in this conversation. Read the Italian on the left and follow the instructions to make your reply. Then test yourself by concealing the answers with the cover flap.

⑤ *parking lot*

Dica? deekah *Can I help you?* Ask: *Is there a library in town?*	**C'è una biblioteca in città?** chay oonah beebleeotaykah een cheettah
No, ma c'è un museo. noh, mah chay oon moozayoh *No, but there's a museum.* Ask: *How do I get to the museum?*	**E per andare al museo?** ay per andaray al moozayoh
È nella piazza. ay nellah peeatsah *It's in the square.* Say: *Thank you.*	**Grazie.** gratseeay

⑦ *museum*

1 Warm up

How do you say "to the station"? (pp.40–1)

Say "Take the first left." (pp.40–1)

Ask "Where are you going?" (pp.40–1)

Le indicazioni
Finding your way

You'll often find a town map (**pianta della città**) situated around town, usually near the town hall or tourist office. In the older parts of Italian towns there are often narrow streets in which you will usually find a one-way system in operation. Parking is usually restricted.

2 Useful phrases

Practice these phrases and then test yourself.

Giri a sinistra/destra. jeeree ah seeneestrah/destrah	*Turn left/right.*
A sinistra/destra. ah seeneestrah/destrah	*On the left/right.*
Sempre dritto. sempray dreettoh	*Straight ahead.*
Per andare alla piscina? per andaray allah peesheenah	*How do I get to the swimming pool?*
La prima a sinistra. lah preemah ah seeneestrah	*First left.*
La seconda a destra. lah sekondah ah destrah	*Second right.*

il municipio
eel mooneecheepeeoh
town hall

la zona pedonale
lah tsonah pedonalay
pedestrian zone

Alla piazza giri a sinistra.
allah peeatsah jeeree ah seeneestrah
At the square, turn left.

3 In conversation

C'è un ristorante in città?
chay oon reestorantay een cheettah

Is there a restaurant in town?

Sì, vicino alla stazione.
see, veecheenoh allah statseeonay

Yes, near the station.

E per andare alla stazione?
ay per andaray allah statseeonay

How do I get to the station?

4 Words to remember

Familiarize yourself with these words and test yourself using the flap.

Mi sono persa.
mee sonoh persah
I'm lost.

traffic lights	**il semaforo** eel semaforoh
corner	**l'angolo** *(m)* langoloh
street/road	**la strada** lah stradah
intersection	**l'incrocio** *(m)* leenkrochoh
map	**la pianta** lah peeantah
overpass	**il cavalcavia** eel kavalkaveeah
across from	**davanti a** davantee ah
at the end of the street	**in fondo alla strada** een fondoh allah stradah

il monumento
eel monoomentoh
monument

Dove siamo?
dovay seeahmoh
Where are we?

5 Say it

Turn right at the end of the street.

It's across from the town hall.

It's ten minutes by bus.

Al semaforo giri a sinistra.
al semaforoh jeeree ah seeneestrah

Turn left at the traffic lights.

È lontano?
ay lontanoh

Is it far?

No, cinque minuti a piedi.
noh, cheenkway meenootee ah peeaydee

No, it's five minutes on foot.

Say the days of the week in Italian. (pp.28–9)

How do you say "at six o'clock"? (pp.30–1)

Ask "What time is it?" (pp.30–1)

Il turismo
Sightseeing

Most national museums close on Mondays; a few are open on some public holidays. Many stores close for lunch, especially in small towns, and public buildings and banks are generally closed in the afternoon. Stores often close on Sundays, except in some tourist areas.

2 Words to remember

Familiarize yourself with these words and test yourself using the flap.

la guida lah gweedah	*guidebook*
la tariffa ridotta lah tareefah reedottah	*discount rate*
l'orario di apertura *(m)* lorareeoh dee apertoorah	*opening times*
il giorno festivo eel jornoh festeevoh	*public holiday*
l'entrata libera lentratah leebayrah	*free admission*

la visita guidata
lah veeseetah gweedatah
guided tour

> **■■ Cultural tip** You will be asked to pay an admission fee in most museums, historic buildings, and even some churches. Children ("bambini"), students ("studenti"), or seniors ("pensionati") can ask for the discount rate, which is sometimes available.

3 In conversation

È aperto oggi pomeriggio?
ay apertoh ojjee pomereejjoh

Are you open this afternoon?

Sì, ma chiudiamo alle sei.
see, mah kyoodeeamoh allay say

Yes, but we close at six o'clock.

C'è l'accesso per i disabili?
chay lacchayssoh per ee deezabeelee

Do you have disabled access?

4 Useful phrases

Learn these phrases and then test yourself using the cover flap.

What time do you open/close?	**A che ora aprite/chiudete?** ah kay orah apreetay/keeoodetay
Where are the restrooms?	**Dov'è la toilette?** dovay lah toyeeletay
Is there disabled access?	**C'è l'accesso per i disabili?** chay lacchayssoh per ee deezabeelee

5 Put into practice

Cover the text on the right and complete the dialogue in Italian.

Spiacente. Il museo è chiuso.
speeachentay. eel moozayoh ay keeoozoh
Sorry. The museum is closed.

Ask: Are you open on Mondays?

È aperto il lunedì?
ay apertoh eel loonedee

Sì, ma chiude presto.
see, mah keeooday prestoh
Yes, but we close early.

Ask: What time?

A che ora?
ah kay orah

Sì, là c'è l'ascensore.
see, lah chay lashaynsoray

Yes, there's an elevator over there.

Grazie. Vorrei quattro biglietti.
gratseeay. vorray kwattroh beellyetTee

Thank you. I'd like four admission tickets.

Ecco a Lei. La guida è gratuita.
ekkoh ah lay. lah gweedah ay gratweetah

Here you are. The guidebook is free.

1 Warm up

Say "You're on time." (pp.14–15)

What's the Italian for "ticket"? (pp.38–9)

Say "I am going to New York." (pp.40–1)

All'aeroporto
At the airport

Although the airport environment is largely universal, it is sometimes useful to be able to understand key words and phrases in Italian. It's a good idea to make sure you have a few one-euro coins when you arrive at the airport; you may need to pay for a baggage cart.

2 Words to remember

Familiarize yourself with these words and test yourself using the flap.

il check-in eel chekeen	*check-in*	
le partenze lay partentsay	*departures*	
gli arrivi lly arreevee	*arrivals*	
la dogana lah doganah	*customs*	
il controllo passaporti eel kontrolloh passaportee	*passport control*	
il terminale eel termeenal	*terminal*	
l'uscita loosheetah	*gate*	
il numero del volo eel noomeroh del voloh	*flight number*	

Qual è l'uscita del volo per Roma?
kwalay loosheetah del voloh per rohmah
Which gate does the flight to Rome leave from?

3 Useful phrases

Learn these phrases and then test yourself using the cover flap.

Il volo da Alghero è in orario? eel voloh dah algayroh ay een orareeoh	*Is the flight from Alghero on time?*	
Non trovo i miei bagagli. non trovoh ee mee-ayee bagallyee	*I can't find my baggage.*	
Il volo per Londra è in ritardo. eel voloh per londrah ay een reetardoh	*The flight to London is delayed.*	

4 Put into practice

Join in this conversation. Read the Italian on the left and follow the instructions to make your reply. Then test yourself by concealing the answers with the cover flap.

Buonasera. Dica?
bwonasayrah. dikah
Hello. Can I help you?

Ask: Is the flight to Milan on time?

Il volo per Milano è in orario?
eel voloh per meelanoh ay een orareeoh

Sì, signore.
see, seennyoray
Yes, sir.

Ask: Which gate does it leave from?

Qual è l'uscita del volo?
kwalay loosheetah del voloh

5 Match and repeat

Match the numbered items to the Italian words in the panel.

boarding pass ❶
check-in desk ❷
ticket ❸
passport ❹
❺ suitcase   ❻ carry-on luggage   ❼ cart

1 **la carta d'imbarco**
lah kartah deembarkoh

2 **lo sportello del check-in**
loh sportelloh del chekeen

3 **il biglietto**
eel beellyettoh

4 **il passaporto**
eel passaportoh

5 **la valigia**
lah valeejah

6 **il bagaglio a mano**
eel bagallyoh ah manoh

7 **il carrello**
eel karrelloh

Ripassa e ripeti
Review and repeat

1 Places

Name the numbered places in Italian.

❶ *museum* ❷ *town hall* ❸ *bridge*

❹ *square* ❺ *parking lot*

❻ *cathedral*

❼ *downtown*

2 Car parts

Name these car parts in Italian.

windshield ❶

❸ *tire* ❹ *door*

3 Questions

Ask the questions in Italian that match the following answers:

1 Il pullman parte alle otto.

2 Sono tre euro e venti.

3 No grazie, non voglio vino.

4 Il treno parte dal binario sette.

5 Vado a Roma.

6 Sì, il diciotto passa di qui.

7 Il museo è in centro.

3 Questions

1 **A che ora parte il pullman?**
ah kay orah partay eel poolman

2 **Quant'è?**
kwantay

3 **Vuole del vino?**
vwolay del veenoh

4 **Da quale binario parte il treno?**
dah kwalay beenareeoh partay eel trenoh

5 **Dove va?**
dovay vah

6 **Passa di qui il diciotto?**
passah dee kwee eel deechottoh

7 **Dov'è il museo?**
dovay eel moozayoh

4 Verbs

Fill in the blanks with the right form of the verb in brackets.

1 (io) _____ scozzese. (essere)

2 (noi) _____ l'autobus. (prendere)

3 Il treno _____ a Verona. (andare)

4 (loro) _____ tre bambine. (avere)

5 (tu) _____ un tè? (volere)

6 Quanti figli _____ signora? (avere)

2 *turn signal*

MEGANE

5 *bumper*

4 Verbs

1 **sono**
sonoh

2 **prendiamo**
prendeeamoh

3 **va**
vah

4 **hanno**
annoh

5 **vuoi**
vwoee

6 **ha**
ah

Prenotare una camera
Booking a room

In Italy you can stay in a standard **hotel** (or **l'albergo**). There is also the small, family-run hotel (**la pensione**), which is usually cheaper. Another option is a self-service vacation apartment (**l'appartamento per le vacanze**).

2 Useful phrases

Practice these phrases and then test yourself by concealing the Italian on the left with the cover flap.

La colazione è compresa? lah kolatseeonay ay komprezah	*Is breakfast included?*	
Accettate animali domestici? acchayttatay aneemalee domesteechee	*Do you accept pets?*	
C'è il servizio in camera? chay eel sayrveetsyoh een kamayrah	*Is there room service?*	
A che ora devo lasciare la camera? ah kay orah devoh lasharay lah kamayrah	*What time do I have to check out?*	

3 In conversation

Avete una camera?
avetay oonah kamayrah

Do you have any rooms?

Sì, abbiamo una matrimoniale.
see, abbeeamoh oonah matreemoneealay

Yes, we have a double room.

È possibile avere anche un lettino?
ay posseebeelay averay ankay oon letteenoh

Is it possible to get a crib, too?

4 Words to remember

Familiarize yourself with these words and test yourself by concealing the Italian on the right with the cover flap.

La camera ha la vista sul parco?
lah kamayrah ah lah veestah sool parkoh
Does the room have a view over the park?

room	**la camera** lah kamayrah
single room	**la camera singola** lah kamayrah seengolah
double room	**la camera matrimoniale** lah kamayrah matreemoneealay
twin room	**la camera a due letti** lah kamayrah ah dooay layttee
bathroom	**il bagno** eel bannyoh
shower	**la doccia** lah docchah
breakfast	**la colazione** lah kolatseeonay
key	**la chiave** lah keeavay
balcony	**il balcone** eel balkonay

5 Say it

Do you have a single room, please?

For six nights.

Does the room have a balcony?

Cultural tip Generally in a hotel you have to pay extra if you want breakfast, but in a "pensione" it is included in the price. It usually consists of a choice of coffee or tea, pastries and/or bread with jam and butter, cereal, and juice.

Non c'è problema. Per quante notti?
non chay problemah.
per kwantay nottee

No problem. How many nights?

Per tre notti.
per tray nottee

For three nights.

Benissimo. Ecco a Lei la chiave.
beneesseemoh. ekkoh ah lay lah keeavay

Very good. Here's the key.

1 Warm up

How do you say "Is there...?" and "There isn't..."? (pp.48–9)

What does "Dica?" mean? (pp.48–9)

In albergo
In the hotel

Although the larger hotels almost always have private bathrooms, there are still some **pensioni** where you will have to share the facilities. This can also be the case in some youth hostels (**ostelli della gioventù**), where a whole family can stay the night for a very reasonable cost.

2 Match and repeat

Match the numbered items in this hotel bedroom with the Italian text in the panel and test yourself using the cover flap.

1 **il comodino**
 eel komodeenoh

2 **la lampada**
 lah lampadah

3 **lo stereo**
 loh sterayoh

4 **le tende**
 lay tenday

5 **il divano**
 eel deevanoh

6 **il guanciale**
 eel gwanchalay

7 **il cuscino**
 eel kusheenoh

8 **il letto**
 eel lettoh

9 **il copriletto**
 eel kopreelettoh

10 **la coperta**
 lah kopertah

❶ *nightstand*

❷ *lamp*

❸ *stereo system*

❹ *curtains*

❺ *sofa*

❻ *pillow*

❼ *cushion*

❽ *bed*

❾ *bedspread*

❿ *blanket*

🇮🇹 **Cultural tip** You'll find that the price of rooms varies according to the season, especially in tourist resorts. The highest prices are charged during the high season ("l'alta stagione"). Accommodation is generally much cheaper in the low season ("la bassa stagione"). It's a good idea to check before you book.

3 Useful phrases

Learn these phrases and then test yourself using the cover flap.

The room is too cold/hot.

In camera fa troppo freddo/caldo.
een kamayrah fah troppoh freddoh/kaldoh

There are no towels.

Non ci sono gli asciugamani.
non chee sonoh lly ashugamanee

I'd like some soap.

Vorrei del sapone.
vorray del saponay

The shower doesn't work very well.

La doccia non funziona bene.
lah docchah non funtseeonah benay

The elevator is not working.

L'ascensore non funziona.
lashensoray non funtseeonah

4 Put into practice

Cover the text on the right and then complete the dialogue in Italian.

Buonasera. Dica?
bwonasayrah. deekah
Hello. Can I help you?

Say: I'd like some pillows.

Vorrei dei guanciali.
vorray day gwanchalee

La cameriera glieli porta subito.
lah kamereeayrah llyaylee portah soobeetoh
The maid will bring you some right away.

Say: And the television doesn't work.

E la televisione non funziona.
ay lah televeezeeonay non foontseeonah

Ask "Can I?" (pp.34–5)

What is Italian for "the shower"? (pp.60–1)

Say "I'd like some towels." (pp.60–1)

In campeggio
At the campground

Camping is popular in Italy among Italians and visitors. Campgrounds are numerous and well organized. The local tourist office can usually provide a list of official campgrounds in the area where you plan to stay. Respect any signs announcing **campeggio vietato** (*camping forbidden*).

2 Useful phrases

Learn these phrases and then test yourself by concealing the Italian with the cover flap.

È possibile noleggiare una bicicletta? ay posseebeelay nolayjjaray oonah beecheeklettah	*Can I rent a bicycle?*
L'acqua è potabile? lahkkwah ay potabeelay	*Is this drinking water?*
È permesso accendere i falò? ay permessoh acchenderay ee faloh	*Are campfires allowed?*
È proibito giocare a pallone. ay proeebeetoh jokaray ah pallonay	*Ball games are forbidden.*

il telo protettivo —
eel teloh protetteevoh
flysheet

Il campeggio è tranquillo.
eel kampayjjoh ay trankweelloh
The campground is quiet.

la direzione del campeggio
lah deeraytseeonay del kampayjjoh
campground office

i rifiuti
ee reefeeootee
trash can

3 In conversation

Vorremmo una piazzola per tre notti.
vorremmoh oonah peeatsolah per tray nottee

I need a site for three nights.

Ce n'è una vicino alla piscina.
chay nay oonah veecheenoh allah peesheenah

There's one near the swimming pool.

Quant'è?
kwantay

How much is it?

4 Words to remember

Familiarize yourself with these words and test yourself using the flap.

5 Say it

I need a site for four nights.

Can I rent a tent?

Where's the electrical hookup?

tent	**la tenda** lah tendah
camper trailer	**la roulotte** lah roolott
camper van	**il camper** eel kamper
air mattress	**il materassino gonfiabile** eel matayraseenoh gonfeeyabeelay
sleeping bag	**il sacco a pelo** eel sakkoh ah peloh
site	**la piazzola** lah peeatsolah
campfire	**il falò** eel faloh
drinking water	**l'acqua potabile** *(f)* lahkkwah potabeelay
garbage	**l'immondizia** *(f)* leemmondeetseeah
showers	**le docce** lay docchay
flashlight	**la torcia** lah torchah
backpack	**lo zaino** loh tsa-eenoh
stove fuel	**il gas da campeggio** eel gas dah kampayjjoh

i bagni
ee banyee
restrooms

la presa di corrente
lah praysah dee korrentay
electrical hookup

la corda
lah kordah
guy rope

il pichetto
eel peekettoh
peg

Cinquanta euro, una notte anticipata.
cheenkwantah ehooroh, oonah nottay anteecheepatah

Fifty euros, one night in advance.

È possibile affittare un barbecue?
ay posseebeelay affeettaray oon barbeku

Can I rent a barbecue grill?

Sì, ma deve versare una cauzione.
see, mah devay versaray oonah kaootseeonay

Yes, but you must pay a deposit.

Descrizione
Descriptions

Adjectives are words used to describe people, things, and places. In Italian you generally put the adjective after the thing it describes—for example, **una camera singola** (*a single room*), but you will sometimes see them placed before—for example, **una bella donna** (*a beautiful woman*).

2 Words to remember

Adjectives usually change depending on whether the thing described is masculine, feminine, masculine plural, or feminine plural. In most cases, adjectives end in "o" for masculine singular words and "a" for the feminine. Plural endings are "i" for masculine and "e" for feminine. Some adjectives end in "e" for the masculine and the feminine, changing to "i" in the plural, others never change.

grande granday	*big, large*
piccolo/piccola peekkoloh/peekkolah	*small*
alto/alta altoh/altah	*high, tall*
basso/bassa bassoh/bassah	*short*
caldo/calda kaldoh/kaldah	*hot*
freddo/fredda freddoh/freddah	*cold*
buono/buona bwonoh/bwonah	*good*
cattivo/cattiva katteevoh/katteevah	*bad*
lento/lenta lentoh/lentah	*slow*
veloce velochay	*fast*
duro/dura dooroh/doorah	*hard*
morbido/morbida morbeedoh/morbeedah	*soft*
bello/bella belloh/bellah	*beautiful*
brutto/brutta broottoh/broottah	*ugly*

Le montagne sono alte.
lay montanyay sonoh altay
The mountains are high.

La chiesa è vecchia.
lah keeayzah eh vekkeeah
The church is old.

Il paese è molto bello.
eel pahesay ay moltoh belloh
The village is very beautiful.

3 Useful phrases

You can emphasize a description by using **molto** (*very*), **troppo** (*too*), or **più** (*more*) before the adjective.

The coffee is cold.	**Il caffè è freddo.** eel kaffay ay freddoh

My room is very noisy.	**La mia camera è molto rumorosa.** lah mee-ah kamayrah ay moltoh roomorosah

The car is too small.	**L'auto è troppo piccola.** la-ootoh ay troppoh peekkolah

I'd like a softer bed.	**Vorrei un letto più morbido.** vorray oon lettoh peeoo morbeedoh

4 Put into practice

Join in this conversation. Cover up the text on the right and complete the dialogue in Italian. Check and repeat if necessary.

Ecco la camera. ekkoh lah kamayrah *Here is the bedroom.* *Say: The view is very beautiful.*	**La vista è molto bella.** lah veestah ay moltoh bellah

Il bagno è là. eel bannyoh ay lah *The bathroom is over there.* *Say: It is too small.*	**È troppo piccolo.** ay troppoh peekkoloh

Non abbiamo altre camere. non abbeeamoh altray kamayray *We don't have any other rooms.* *Say: We'll take it.*	**La prendiamo.** lah prendeeamoh

Ripassa e ripeti
Review and repeat

1 Adjectives

1 **piccola**
peekkolah

2 **morbido**
morbeedoh

3 **buono**
bwonoh

4 **freddo**
freddoh

5 **grande**
granday

1 Adjectives

Put the word in brackets into Italian using the correct masculine or feminine form.

1 La camera è troppo _____ . (small)

2 Vorrei un guanciale più _____ . (soft)

3 Il caffè è molto _____ . (good)

4 In questo bagno fa _____ . (cold)

5 Vorrei un letto più _____ . (big)

2 Campground

1 **la presa di corrente**
lah praysah dee korrentay

2 **la tenda**
lah tendah

3 **i rifiuti**
ee reefeeootee

4 **la corda**
lah kordah

5 **i bagni**
ee banyee

6 **la roulotte**
lah roolott

2 Campground

Name these items you might find in a campground.

❶ electrical hookup
❷ tent
❸ trash can
❹ guy rope

Risposte
Answers
Cover with flap.

3 At the hotel

You are booking a room in a hotel. Follow the conversation, replying in Italian following the English prompts.

Buongiorno.
1 *Do you have a double room?*

Sì. Per quante notti?
2 *Three nights. Do you accept pets?*

Certo.
3 *Is breakfast included?*

No. Sono cinque euro.
4 *That's fine. We'll take it.*

3 At the hotel

1 **Avete una camera matrimoniale?**
avetay oonah kamerah matreemonyalay

2 **Tre notti. Accettate animali domestici?**
tray nottee. acchayttatay aneemalee domesteechee

3 **La colazione è compresa?**
lah kolatseeonay ay komprezah

4 **Va bene. La prendiamo.**
vah benay. lah prendeeamoh

5 restrooms

6 camper trailer

4 Negatives

Make these sentences negative using the correct form of the verb in brackets.

1 (io) _____ figli. (avere)

2 (Lei) _____ a Genova domani. (andare)

3 (lui) _____ vino. (volere)

4 (io) _____ lo zucchero nel caffè. (volere)

5 La camera _____ molto bella. (essere)

4 Negatives

1 **non ho**
non oh

2 **non va**
non vah

3 **non vuole**
non vwolay

4 **non voglio**
non vollyoh

5 **non è**
non ay

1 Warm up

Ask "How do I get to the station?" (pp.50–1)

Say "Turn left at the traffic lights," and "The station is across from the café." (pp.50–1)

I negozi
Shops

Small, traditional specialized shops are still very common in Italy. But you can also find big supermarkets and shopping malls on the outskirts of cities. Local markets selling fresh, local produce can be found everywhere. You can find out the market day at the tourist office.

2 Match and repeat

Match the shops numbered 1–9 below and right to the Italian in the panel. Then test yourself using the cover flap.

1 **la panetteria**
   lah panettayreeah

2 **la pasticceria**
   lah pastee-chayreeah

3 **gli alimentari**
   llyaleementaree

4 **la salumeria**
   lah saloomay-reeah

5 **il tabaccaio**
   eel tabakkaeeoh

6 **la libreria**
   lah leebrayreeah

7 **la pescheria**
   lah payskayreeah

8 **la macelleria**
   lah machayllay-reeah

9 **la banca**
   lah bankah

1 *bread shop*

2 *bakery*

4 *delicatessen*

5 *tobacconist*

7 *fishmonger*

8 *butcher shop*

Cultural tip Although most Italian pharmacies also sell cosmetics and toiletries, the best shop in which to buy these items is "la profumeria." Some are very upmarket and offer a wider range of brands. "Il tabaccaio" (tobacconist) is the only licensed outlet for cigarettes and stamps (except the post office in the case of stamps). Sometimes you will find a tobacconist counter within the premises of a bar.

3 Words to remember

Familiarize yourself with these words and then test yourself.

Dov'è il fioraio?
dovay eel feeoraeeoh
Where is the florist?

dairy	**la latteria** lah lattereeah
wine store	**l'enoteca** *(f)* laynotekah
antique shop	**l'antiquario** *(m)* lanteekwareeoh
hairdresser	**il parrucchiere** eel parrookyayray
jeweler	**la gioielleria** la joyayllereeah
post office	**le poste** lay postay
leather goods shop	**la pelletteria** lah pellettereeah
travel agent	**l'agenzia di viaggi** lajentseeah dee veeajjee
shoe repairer	**il calzolaio** eel kaltsolaeeoh

3 grocery store

6 bookstore

9 bank

4 Useful phrases

Familiarize yourself with these phrases.

Where is the hairdresser?	**Dov'è il parrucchiere?** dovay eel parrookyayray
Where do I pay?	**Dove pago?** dovay pagoh
I'm just looking, thank you.	**Do solo un'occhiata, grazie.** doh soloh oonokyatah, gratseeay
Do you sell phone cards?	**Avete schede telefoniche?** avetay skayday telayfoneekay
Can I exchange this?	**Posso cambiare questo?** possoh kambeearay kwestoh
Can you give me the receipt?	**Mi dà lo scontrino?** mee dah loh skontreenoh
I'd like to place an order	**Vorrei fare un'ordinazione.** vorray faray oonordeenatseeonay

5 Say it

Where is the bank?

Do you sell cheese?

Where do I pay?

Al mercato
At the market

Italy uses the metric system of weights and measures. You need to ask for produce in kilograms—**chili** for short—or grams. Some larger items tend to be priced individually, **l'uno** (each). In many Italian markets you will find foodstuffs and also stands selling clothing and household goods.

2 Match and repeat

Match the numbered items in this scene with the text in the panel.

1   **il finocchio**
    eel feenokeeoh

2   **il cavolfiore**
    eel kavolfeeoray

3   **la lattuga**
    lah lattoogah

4   **i peperoni**
    ee paypaironee

5   **le patate**
    lay patatay

6   **l'aglio** *(m)*
    lalyoh

7   **i pomodori**
    ee pomodoree

8   **gli asparagi**
    lly asparajee

❶ *fennel*

❻ *garlic*   *tomatoes* ❼

❺ *potatoes*   *asparagus* ❽

3 In conversation

Vorrei dei pomodori.
vorray day pomodoree

I'd like some tomatoes.

Quanti chili?
kwantee keelee

How many kilos?

Due chili, per favore.
dooay keelee, per favoray

Two kilos, please.

Cultural tip Italy uses the European currency, the euro. This is divided into 100 cents, which the Italians call "centesimi." You will usually hear the price given as: dieci euro e venti (€10.20), sei euro e novantanove (€6,99), etc. Italians use a comma for the decimal point.

4 Useful phrases

Learn these phrases. Then conceal the answers on the right using the cover flap. Read the English under the pictures and say the phrase in Italian as shown on the right.

2 *cauliflower*

3 *lettuce*

4 *peppers*

Quel formaggio è troppo caro.
kwel formajjoh ay troppoh karoh

That cheese is too expensive.

Quanto costa quello lì?
kwantoh kostah kwelloh lee

How much is that one?

5 Say it

Three kilos of potatoes, please.

The peppers are too expensive.

How much is the lettuce?

Basta così.
bastah kosee

That's all.

Altro, signore?
altroh, seennyoray

Anything else, sir?

Basta così, grazie. Quant'è?
bastah kozee, gratseeay. kwantay

That's all, thank you. How much?

Due euro e cinquanta.
dooay ayooroh ay cheenkwantah

Two euros fifty.

1 Warm up

What are these items that you could buy in a supermarket? (pp.24–5)

la carne
il pesce
il formaggio
il succo di frutta
il vino
l'acqua

Al supermercato
At the supermarket

Prices in supermarkets are usually lower than in small shops. They offer all kinds of products, with larger out-of-town **ipermercati** (*large supermarkets*) carrying clothes, household goods, garden furniture, and home improvement products. They may also stock regional products.

2 Match and repeat

Look at the numbered items and match them to the Italian words in the panel on the left.

1 **gli articoli per la casa**
lly arteekolee per lah kazah

2 **la frutta**
lah froottah

3 **le bibite**
lay beebeetay

4 **i piatti pronti**
ee pyattee prontee

5 **i cosmetici**
ee kosmeteechee

6 **i latticini**
ee latteecheenee

7 **la verdura**
lah verdoorah

8 **i surgelati**
ee soorjelatee

household products ❶

fruit ❷

drinks ❸

prepared meals ❹

vegetables ❼

frozen foods ❽

Cultural tip It is not usually possible to take unweighed fruit and vegetables sold by the kilo directly to the supermarket checkout. There is usually a self-service weighing machine.

3 Useful phrases

Learn these phrases and then test yourself using the cover flap.

May I have a bag, please?	**Posso avere un sacchetto, per favore?** possoh avayray oon sakkayttoh, per favoray

Where is the liquor aisle?	**Qual è la fila delle bibite?** kwalay lah feelah dellay beebeetay

Where is the checkout, please?	**Dov'è la cassa?** dovay lah kassah

Please type in your PIN.	**Può battere il pin.** pwoh battayray eel pin

4 Words to remember

Learn these words and then test yourself using the cover flap.

5 *beauty products*

6 *dairy products*

bread	**il pane** eel panay
milk	**il latte** eel lattay
butter	**il burro** eel boorroh
ham	**il prosciutto** eel proshoottoh
salt	**il sale** eel salay
pepper	**il pepe** eel paypay
toilet paper	**la carta igienica** lah kartah eejeneekah
diapers	**i pannolini** ee pannoleenee
dishwashing liquid	**il detersivo per i piatti** eel deterseevoh per ee pyattee

5 Say it

Where's the dairy products aisle?

May I have some ham, please?

Where are the frozen foods?

1 Warm up

Say "I'd like…".
(pp.22–3)

Ask "Do you have…?"
(pp.14–15)

Say "38," "42," and
"46." (pp.30–1)

Say "big" and
"small." (pp.64–5)

Scarpe e abbigliamento
Clothes and shoes

Clothes and shoes are measured in metric sizes. Even allowing for conversion of sizes, Italian clothes tend to be cut very small. Note that clothes size is **la taglia** but shoe size is **il numero**.

2 Match and repeat

Match the numbered items of clothing to the Italian words in the panel on the left. Test yourself using the cover flap.

1 **la camicia**
lah kameechah

2 **la cravatta**
lah kravattah

3 **la giacca**
lah jakkah

4 **la tasca**
lah taskah

5 **la manica**
lah maneekah

6 **i pantaloni**
ee pantalonee

7 **la gonna**
lah gonnah

8 **i collant**
ee kollant

9 **le scarpe**
lay skarpay

shirt ❶

tie ❷

jacket ❸

pocket ❹

sleeve ❺

pants ❻

Cultural tip Like most of Europe, Italy uses the continental system of sizes. Italian dress sizes usually range from 36 (US 6) through to 48 (US 14) and shoe sizes from 37 (US 5 ½) to 46 (US 12). For men's shirts, a size 41 is a 16-inch collar, 43 is a 17-inch collar, and 45 is an 18-inch collar.

3 Useful phrases

Learn these phrases and then test yourself using the cover flap.

Do you have a larger size? — **Ha la taglia più grande?**
ah lah tallyah peeoo granday

It's not what I want. — **Non è quello che cerco.**
non ay kwelloh kay cherkoh

I'll take the pink one. — **Prendo quella rosa.**
prendoh kwellah rozah

4 Words to remember

Colors are adjectives (see p.64) and in most cases have a masculine and a feminine form. The latter is usually formed by changing the final "o" to an "a."

red	**rosso/rossa** rossoh/rossah
white	**bianco/bianca** byankoh/byankah
blue	**azzurro/azzurra** adzoorroh/adzoorrah
yellow	**giallo/gialla** jalloh/jallah
green	**verde** verday
black	**nero/nera** neroh/nerah

❼ *skirt*

❽ *pantyhose*

❾ *shoes*

5 Say it

What shoe size?

I'll take the black one.

I'd like a 38.

Do you have a smaller size?

Risposte
Answers
Cover with flap

Ripassa e ripeti
Review and repeat

1 Market

Market

Name the numbered vegetables in Italian.

❶ *fennel* *lettuce* ❹ *cauliflower* ❺

❷ *garlic* ❸ *tomatoes* ❻ *asparagus*

1 **il finocchio**
eel feenokkeeoh

2 **l'aglio**
lalyoh

3 **i pomodori**
ee pomodoree

4 **la lattuga**
lah lattoogah

5 **il cavolfiore**
eel kavolfeeoray

6 **gli asparagi**
lly asparajee

2 Description

Description

What do these sentences mean?

1 **Queste scarpe sono troppo care.**

2 **La mia camera è molto piccola.**

3 **Vorrei una taglia più grande.**

1 *These shoes are too expensive.*

2 *My room is very small.*

3 *I'd like a bigger size.*

3 Stores

Stores

Name the numbered stores in Italian.
Then check your answers.

❶ *bread shop* ❷ *grocery store* ❸ *bookstore*

❹ *fishmonger* ❺ *bakery* ❻ *butcher shop*

1 **la panetteria**
lah panettayreeah

2 **gli alimentari**
llyaleementaree

3 **la libreria**
lah leebrayreeah

4 **la pescheria**
lah payskayreeah

5 **la pasticceria**
lah pasteechayreeah

6 **la macelleria**
lah machayllayreeah

Supermarket

What is the Italian for the numbered product categories?

1 *household products*

2 *beauty products*

3 *drinks*

4 *dairy products*

5 *frozen foods*

Supermarket

1 **gli articoli per la casa**
lly arteekolee per lah kazah

2 **i cosmetici**
ee kosmeteechee

3 **le bibite**
lay beebeetay

4 **i latticini**
ee latteecheenee

5 **i surgelati**
ee soorjelatee

Museum

Follow this conversation replying in Italian following the English prompts.

Buongiorno, dica?
1 *I'd like five tickets.*

Sono settanta euro.
2 *That's very expensive! Two are children.*

Non ci sono riduzioni per bambini.
3 *How much is a guide?*

Quindici euro.
4 *Five tickets, then, and a guide.*

Ottantacinque euro.
5 *Here you are. Where are the restrooms?*

Là, a destra.
6 *Thank you.*

Museum

1 **Vorrei cinque biglietti.**
vorray cheenkway beellyettee

2 **È molto caro! Due sono bambini.**
ay moltoh karoh. dooay sonoh bambeenee

3 **Quanto costa la guida?**
kwantoh kostah lah gweedah

4 **Allora cinque biglietti e una guida.**
allorah cheenkway beellyettee ay oonah gweedah

5 **Ecco a lei. Dove sono le toilette?**
ekkoh ah lay. dovay sonoh lay twaletay

6 **Grazie.**
gratseeay

1 Warm up

Ask "which platform?" (pp.38–9)

What is the Italian for the following family members: sister, brother, mother, father, son, and daughter? (pp.10–11)

Il lavoro
Jobs

Some occupations have commonly used feminine forms, for example, **l'infermiere** (*male nurse*) and **l'infermiera** (*female nurse*). Others stay the same **il/la giornalista** (*male/female journalist*). To describe your job, you don't always use **un** (*a*); you say, for example, **sono medico** (*I'm a doctor*).

2 Words to remember: jobs

Familiarize yourself with these words and test yourself using the flap. The feminine alternative is shown.

medico medeekoh	*doctor*
dentista denteestah	*dentist*
infermiere/a eenfermyeray/ah	*nurse*
insegnante eensennyantay	*teacher*
ragioniere/a rajonyeray/ah	*accountant*
avvocato avvokatoh	*lawyer*
grafico/a grafeekoh/ah	*designer*
consulente finanziario konsoolentay feenantseearyoh	*financial consultant*
segretario/a segretaryoh/ah	*secretary*
commerciante kommerchantay	*shopkeeper*
elettricista elettreecheestah	*electrician*
idraulico eedraooleekoh	*plumber*
cuoco/a kwokoh/ah	*cook/chef*
libero/a professionista leeberoh/ah professyoneestah	*self-employed*

Sono un idraulico.
sonoh oon
eedraooleekoh
I'm a plumber.

È studentessa.
ay stoodentessah
She is a student.

3 Put into practice

Join in this conversation. Use the cover flap to conceal the text on the right and complete the dialogue in Italian.

Che lavoro fa?
kay lavoroh fah
What do you do?

Say: *I am a financial consultant.*

Sono consulente finanziario.
sonoh konsoolentay feenantseearyoh

Per quale azienda lavora?
per kwalay adzyendah lavorah
What company do you work for?

Say: *I'm self-employed.*

Sono libero professionista.
sonoh leeberoh professyoneestah

Interessante!
eenteressantay
How interesting!

Ask: *What is your profession?*

E Lei che lavoro fa?
ay lay kay lavoroh fah

Sono dentista.
sonoh denteestah
I'm a dentist.

Say: *My sister is a dentist, too.*

Anche mia sorella è dentista.
ankay mee-ah sorellah ay denteestah

4 Words to remember: workplace

Familiarize yourself with these words and test yourself.

La sede centrale è a Napoli.
lah seday chentralay ay ah napolee
Headquarters is in Naples.

headquarters	**la sede centrale** lah seday chentralay
branch	**la filiale** lah feelyalay
department	**il reparto** eel repartoh
office worker	**l'impiegato/a** leempyegatoh/ah
manager	**il direttore/la direttrice** eel deerettoray/lah deerettreechay

1 Warm up

Practice different ways of introducing yourself in different situations (pp.8–9). Mention your name, occupation, and any other information you'd like to volunteer (pp.12–13, pp.14–15).

L'ufficio
The office

An office environment or business situation has its own vocabulary in any language, but there are many items for which the terminology is virtually universal. Be aware that Italian computer keyboards may have a different layout from the standard US "QWERTY" convention.

2 Words to remember

Familiarize yourself with these words. Read them aloud several times and try to memorize them. Conceal the Italian with the cover flap and test yourself.

il computer eel komputer	*computer*
il mouse eel maoos	*mouse*
l'email *(f)* leemayl	*email*
internet *(f)* eenternet	*Internet*
la password lah password	*password*
la segreteria telefonica lah segretereeah telayfoneekah	*voicemail*
il fax eel fax	*fax machine*
la fotocopiatrice lah fotokopyatreechay	*photocopier*
l'agenda *(f)* lajendah	*planner*
il biglietto da visita eel beellyettoh dah veeseetah	*business card*
la riunione lah reeoonyonay	*meeting*
la conferenza lah konferentsah	*conference*
l'ordine del giorno *(m)* lordeenay del jornoh	*agenda*

❶ *lamp*

❹ *screen*

❷ *stapler*

❸ *telephone*

❿ *pen*

⓫ *notepad*

⓬ *drawer*

3 Useful phrases

Learn these phrases and then test yourself using the cover flap.

I need to make some photocopies.

Ho bisogno di fare delle fotocopie.
oh beezonnyoh dee faray dellay fotokopyay

I'd like to make an appointment.

Vorrei fissare un appuntamento.
vorray feessaray oon appoontamentoh

I want to send an email.

Voglio mandare un'email.
vollyoh mandaray oon eemayl

4 Match and repeat

Match the numbered items to the Italian words on the right.

5 *keyboard*

6 *laptop*

printer **9**

7 *desk*

8 *clock*

13 *swivel chair*

1 **la lampada**
lah lampadah

2 **la spillatrice**
lah speellatreechay

3 **il telefono**
eel telayfonoh

4 **lo schermo**
loh skayrmoh

5 **la tastiera**
lah tastyerah

6 **il computer portatile**
eel komputer portateelay

7 **la scrivania**
lah skreevaneeah

8 **l'orologio** *(m)*
lorolojoh

9 **la stampante**
lah stampantay

10 **la penna**
lah pennah

11 **il bloc-notes**
eel bloknotays

12 **il cassetto**
eel kassettoh

13 **la sedia girevole**
lah sedya jeerayvolay

5 Say it

I'd like to arrange a meeting.

I need to send a fax.

Do you have a laptop?

1 Warm up

Say "How interesting!" (pp.78–9), "library" (pp.48–9), and "appointment." (pp.32–3)

Ask "What is your profession?" and answer "I'm an accountant." (pp.78–9)

Il mondo accademico
Academic world

Italian students may take a short degree course, **la laurea breve**. There is also a longer course, **la laurea**, equivalent to a master's degree. The title **dottore** or **dottoressa** is used by all graduates and most professionals.

2 Useful phrases

Learn these phrases and then test yourself using the cover flap.

Di cosa si occupa? dee kozah see okkoopah	*What is your field?*	
Mi occupo di ricerca scientifica. mee okkoopoh dee reecherkah shenteefeekah	*I am doing scientific research.*	
Sono laureato in legge. sonoh laooreatoh een lejjay	*I have a degree in law.*	
Tengo una conferenza sull'architettura moderna. tayngoh oonah konferentsah soollarkeetettoorah modernah	*I am giving a lecture on modern architecture.*	

3 In conversation

Buongiorno, sono la professoressa Lanzi. bwonjornoh, sonoh lah professoressah lantsee

Hello, I'm Professor Lanzi.

Dove insegna? dovay eensennyah

Where do you teach?

Insegno all'università di Pisa. eensennyoh allooneeverseetah dee pisah

I teach at the University of Pisa.

4 Words to remember

Familiarize yourself with these words and then test yourself.

conference/lecture	**la conferenza** lah konferentsah
seminar	**il seminario** eel semeenaryoh
conference room	**la sala conferenze** lah salah konferentsay
lecture hall	**l'aula delle lezioni** *(f)* laoolah dellay letseeonee
exhibition	**la mostra** lah mostrah
associate professor	**il professore universitario/la professoressa universitaria** eel professoray ooneeverseetareeoh/lah professoressah ooneeverseetaryah
medicine	**la medicina** lah medeecheenah
science	**la scienza** lah schentsah
literature	**la letteratura** lah letteratoorah
engineering	**l'ingegneria** *(f)* leenjennyereeah
information technology	**l'informatica** *(f)* leenformateekah

Abbiamo uno stand alla fiera commerciale.
abbyamoh oonoh stend allah fyerah kommerchalay
We have a stand at the trade fair.

5 Say it

I'm doing research in medicine.

I have a degree in literature.

She's the professor.

Di cosa si occupa?
dee kozah see okkoopah

What's your field?

Di fisica. Mi occupo di ricerca.
dee feeseekah. mee okkoopoh dee reecherkah

Physics. I'm doing research.

Interessante!
eenteressantay

How interesting!

1 Warm up

Ask "Can I...?"
(pp.34–5)

Say "I want to send an email." (pp.80–1)

Say "I'd like to make an appointment." (pp.80–1)

I contatti commerciali
In business

You will make a good impression if you make the effort to begin a meeting with a few words in Italian, even if your vocabulary is limited. After that, all parties will probably be happy to continue in English.

2 Words to remember

Familiarize yourself with these words and then test yourself by concealing the Italian with the cover flap.

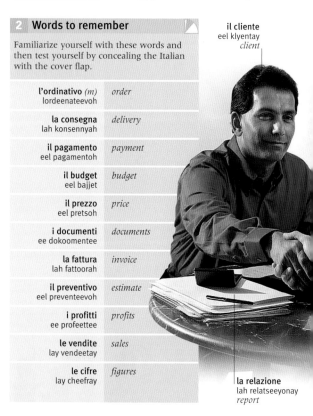

il cliente
eel klyentay
client

l'ordinativo *(m)* lordeenateevoh		*order*
la consegna lah konsennyah		*delivery*
il pagamento eel pagamentoh		*payment*
il budget eel bajjet		*budget*
il prezzo eel pretsoh		*price*
i documenti ee dokoomentee		*documents*
la fattura lah fattoorah		*invoice*
il preventivo eel preventeevoh		*estimate*
i profitti ee profeettee		*profits*
le vendite lay vendeetay		*sales*
le cifre lay cheefray		*figures*

la relazione
lah relatseeyonay
report

Cultural tip In general, business dealings are formal, but a long lunch with wine is still a feature of doing business in Italy. As a client, you can expect to be taken out to a restaurant, and as a supplier you should consider entertaining your customers.

3 Useful phrases

Practice these phrases. Notice the use of the word **può** (*can you*) as a preface to polite requests.

Firmiamo il contratto?
feermyamoh eel kontrattoh
Shall we sign the contract?

il dirigente
eel deereejentay
executive

Can you send me the contract, please?

Può mandarmi il contratto, per favore?
pwoh mandarmee eel kontrattoh, per favoray

Have we agreed on a price?

Abbiamo fissato il prezzo?
abbeeamoh feessatoh eel pretsoh

When can you make the delivery?

Quando può effettuare la consegna?
kwandoh pwoh effettwaray lah konsennyah

What's the budget?

Quant'è il budget?
kwantay eel bajjet

Can you send me the invoice?

Può mandarmi la fattura?
pwoh mandarmee lah fattoorah

il contratto
eel kontrattoh
contract

4 Say it

Can you send me the estimate?

Have we agreed on a budget?

When can you send me the contract?

Ripassa e ripeti
Review and repeat

1 At the office

1 **la spillatrice**
lah speellatreechay

2 **la lampada**
lah lampadah

3 **il computer portatile**
eel komputer portateelay

4 **la penna**
lah pennah

5 **la scrivania**
lah skreevaneeah

6 **il bloc-notes**
eel bloknotays

7 **l'orologio** *(m)*
lorolojoh

1 At the office

Name these items in Italian.

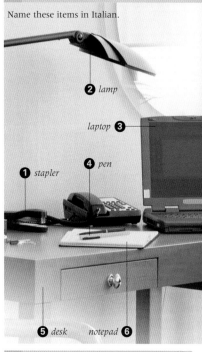

② *lamp*

laptop ③

④ *pen*

① *stapler*

⑤ *desk*   *notepad* ⑥

2 Jobs

1 **medico**
medeekoh

2 **idraulico**
eedraooleekoh

3 **commerciante**
kommerchantay

4 **ragioniere/a**
rajonyeray/ah

5 **studente/essa**
stoodentay/essah

6 **avvocato**
avvokatoh

2 Jobs

What are these jobs in Italian?

1 *doctor*

2 *plumber*

3 *shopkeeper*

4 *accountant*

5 *student*

6 *lawyer*

3 Work

Answer these questions following the English prompts.

Per quale azienda lavora?
1 *Say "I work for myself."*

Dove insegna?
2 *Say "I teach at the University of Pisa."*

Di cosa si occupa?
3 *Say "I'm doing scientific research."*

Quando può mandare il preventivo?
4 *Say "I can send the estimate tomorrow."*

clock ❼

3 Work

1 **Sono libero professionista.**
sonoh leeberoh professyoneestah

2 **Insegno all'università di Pisa.**
eensennyoh allooneeverseetah dee pisah

3 **Mi occupo di ricerca scientifica.**
mee okkoopoh dee reecherkah sheenteefeekah

4 **Posso mandare il preventivo domani.**
possoh mandaray eel preventeevoh domanee

4 How much?

Answer the question with the price shown in brackets.

1 **Quant'è un caffè?** (€1,80)

2 **Quanto costa la camera?** (€47)

3 **Quanto costa un chilo di pomodori?** (€1,25)

4 **Quanto costa una piazzola per tre giorni?** (€50)

4 How much?

1 **Un euro e ottanta**
oon ayooroh ay ottantah

2 **Quarantasette euro**
kwarantasettay ayooroh

3 **Un euro e venticinque**
oon ayooroh ay venteecheenkway

4 **Cinquanta euro**
cheenkwantah ayooroh

1 Warm up

Say "I'm allergic to nuts." (pp.24–5)

Say the verb "avere" (to have) in all its forms (io, tu, Lei, lui/lei, noi, voi, loro) (pp.14–15).

In farmacia
At the pharmacy

Italian pharmacists study for over four years to get their licenses, and they can give advice about minor health problems and are permitted to dispense a wide variety of medicines, even giving injections, if necessary. There is a duty pharmacist (**farmacia di turno**) in most towns.

2 Match and repeat

Match the numbered items to the Italian words in the panel on the left and test yourself using the cover flap.

1   **la fascia**
    lah fasheeah

2   **lo sciroppo**
    loh sheeroppoh

3   **le gocce**
    lay gocchay

4   **il cerotto**
    eel chayrottoh

5   **l'iniezione** *(f)*
    leenyetsyonay

6   **la pomata**
    lah pomatah

7   **la supposta**
    làh sooppostah

8   **la compressa**
    lah kompressah

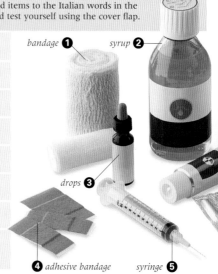

bandage ❶   *syrup* ❷

drops ❸

❹ *adhesive bandage*   *syringe* ❺

3 In conversation

Buongiorno. Dica?
bwonjornoh. deekah

Hello. What would you like?

Ho mal di pancia.
oh mal dee panchah

I have a stomachache.

Ha anche la diarrea?
ah ankay lah deearreah

Do you also have diarrhea?

4 Words to remember

Familiarize yourself with these words and test yourself using the flap.

Ho mal di testa.
oh mal dee testah
I have a headache.

headache	**mal di testa**	mal dee testah
stomachache	**mal di pancia**	mal dee panchah
diarrhea	**la diarrea**	lah deearreah
cold	**il raffreddore**	eel raffreddoray
cough	**la tosse**	lah tossay
sunburn	**l'eritema solare** *(m)*	lereetemah solaray
toothache	**mal di denti**	mal dee dentee

6 Say it

I have a cold.

Do you have that as an ointment?

Do you have a cough?

6 *ointment*

7 *suppository*

8 *tablet*

5 Useful phrases

Learn these phrases and then test yourself using the cover flap.

I have a sunburn.	**Ho l'eritema solare.**	oh lereetemah solaray
Do you have that as a syrup?	**Lo ha in sciroppo?**	loh ah een sheeroppoh
I'm allergic to penicillin.	**Sono allergico/a alla penicillina.**	sonoh allerjeekoh/ah allah peneecheelleenah

No, ma ho mal di testa.
noh, mah oh mal dee testah

No, but I have a headache.

Prenda questo.
prendah kwestoh

Take this.

Lo ha in compresse?
loh ah een kompressay

Do you have that as tablets?

1 Warm up

Say " I have a toothache" and "I have a sunburn." (pp.88–9)

Say the Italian for "red," "green," "black," and "yellow." (pp.74–5)

Il corpo
The body

A common phrase for talking about aches and pains is **mi fa male il/la...** (*my ... hurts*). Another useful expression is **ho un dolore a...** (*I have a pain in...*). Note that **a** joins with the definite article (*the*) to produce these combinations: **il (al)**, **lo (allo)**, **la (alla)**, **gli (agli)**, **i (ai)**, and **le (alle)**.

2 Match and repeat: body

Match the numbered parts of the body with the list on the left. Test yourself by using the cover flap.

1	la mano	*hand* ❶
	lah manoh	
2	la testa	*head* ❷
	lah testah	
3	la spalla	*shoulder* ❸
	la spallah	
4	il gomito	❹ *elbow*
	eel gomeetoh	
5	i capelli	❺ *hair*
	ee kapellee	
6	il braccio	❻ *arm*
	eel brachoh	
7	il collo	❼ *neck*
	eel kolloh	
8	il petto	❽ *chest*
	eel pettoh	
9	lo stomaco	❾ *stomach*
	loh stomakoh	
10	la gamba	❿ *leg*
	lah gambah	
11	il ginocchio	⓫ *knee*
	eel jeenokkyoh	
12	il piede	⓬ *foot*
	eel pyeday	

3 Match and repeat: face

Match the numbered facial features with the list on the right.

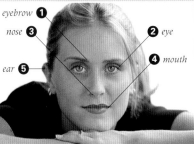

eyebrow **1**

nose **3**

2 *eye*

4 *mouth*

ear **5**

1 **il sopracciglio**
   eel sopracheelyoh

2 **l'occhio** *(m)*
   lokkeeoh

3 **il naso**
   eel nasoh

4 **la bocca**
   lah bokkah

5 **l'orecchio** *(m)*
   lorekkyoh

4 Useful phrases

Learn these phrases and then test yourself using the cover flap.

	My back hurts.	**Mi fa male la schiena.** mee fah malay lah skyenah
	I have a rash on my arm.	**Ho un arrossamento sul braccio.** oh oon arrossamentoh sool brachoh
	I don't feel well.	**Non mi sento bene.** non mee sentoh benay

5 Put into practice

Join in this conversation and test yourself using the cover flap.

Cosa c'è?
kozah chay
What's the matter?

Say: I don't feel well.

Non mi sento bene.
non mee sentoh benay

Dove ti fa male?
dovay ti fah malay
Where does it hurt?

Say: I have a pain in my shoulder.

Ho un dolore alla spalla.
oh oon doloray allah spallah

1 Warm up

Say "I have a headache." (pp.88–9)

Now, say "He needs some ointment." (pp.88–9)

What is the Italian for "I don't have a son." (pp.10–15)

Dal medico
At the doctor's

Unless it's an emergency, you'll have to make an appointment with the doctor and pay when you leave. You may be able to reclaim the cost if you have medical insurance. Find the names and addresses of local doctors from **il municipio** (*town hall*), or ask at a local pharmacy.

2 Useful phrases you may hear

Learn these phrases and then test yourself using the cover flap to conceal the Italian on the left.

Non è grave. non ay gravay	*It's not serious.*
Deve fare dei controlli. devay faray day kontrollee	*You need to have tests.*
Ha una frattura. ah oonah frattoorah	*You have a fracture.*
Deve andare all'ospedale. devay andaray allospedalay	*You need to go to the hospital.*

Fa qualche cura?
fah kwalkay koorah
Are you taking any medication?

3 In conversation

Cosa c'è?
kozah chay

What's the matter?

Ho un dolore al petto.
oh oon doloray al pettoh

I have a pain in my chest.

Ora la visito.
orah lah veezeetoh

Now I will examine you.

Cultural tip Before you go to Italy, find out if your health insurance covers emergency medical care in Europe; if it doesn't, purchase a travel medical insurance policy. For an ambulance call 118.

4 Useful phrases you may need to say

Learn these phrases and then test yourself using the cover flap.

I am diabetic.	**Sono diabetico/a.** sonoh deeabeteekoh/ah
I am epileptic.	**Sono epilettico/a.** sonoh epeeletteekoh/ah
I have asthma.	**Sono asmatico/a.** sonoh asmateekoh/ah
I have a heart condition.	**Ho disturbi cardiaci.** oh deestoorbee kardeeachee
I have a fever.	**Ho la febbre.** oh lah febbray
It's urgent.	**È urgente.** ay oorjentay
I'm out of breath.	**Faccio fatica a respirare.** facchyoh fatikah ah respeeraray

Sono incinta.
sonoh eencheentah
I am pregnant.

5 Say it

My son needs to go to the hospital.

It's not urgent.

È grave?
ay gravay

Is it serious?

No, è solo un'indigestione.
noh, ay soloh oon eendeejestyonay

No, you only have indigestion.

Che sollievo!
kay soleeayvoh

What a relief!

1 Warm up

Say "There's an elevator over there." (pp.52–3)

Ask "Do I need...?" (pp.92–3)

What is the Italian for "mouth" and "head"? (pp.90–1)

All'ospedale
At the hospital

It is useful to know a few basic phrases relating to hospitals for use in an emergency or in case you need to visit a friend or colleague in the hospital. Emergency departments will treat all urgent cases free of charge, but citizens of non-EU countries need to sign a payment declaration.

2 Useful phrases

Familiarize yourself with these phrases. Conceal the Italian with the cover flap and test yourself.

Qual è l'orario di visita? kwalay lorareeoh dee veezeetah	*What are the visiting hours?*
Quanto ci vuole? kwantoh chee vwolay	*How long does it take?*
Farà male? farah malay	*Will it hurt?*
Si sdrai sul lettino. see zdraee sool letteenoh	*Please lie down on the bed.*
Non deve mangiare. non devay manjaray	*You must not eat.*
Non muova la testa. non mwovah lah testah	*Don't move your head.*
Apra la bocca. aprah lah bokkah	*Open your mouth.*
Deve fare le analisi del sangue. devay faray lay analeezee del sangway	*You need a blood test.*

la flebo
lah flayboh
intravenous drip

Si sente meglio?
see sentay mellyoh
Are you feeling better?

Dov'è la sala d'aspetto?
dovay lah salah daspettoh
Where is the waiting room?

3 **Words to remember**

Memorize these words and test yourself using the cover flap.

emergency room	**il pronto soccorso** eel prontoh sokkorsoh
children's ward	**il reparto di pediatria** eel repartoh dee pedyatryah
operating room	**la sala operatoria** lah salah operatoreeah
waiting room	**la sala d'aspetto** lah salah daspettoh
corridor	**il corridoio** eel korreedoyoh
stairs	**le scale** lay skalay
elevator	**l'ascensore** *(m)* lashensoray

La radiografia è normale.
lah radeeografeeah ay normalay
The X-ray is normal.

4 **Put into practice**

Join in this conversation. Read the Italian on the left and follow the instructions to make your reply. Then test yourself by hiding the answers with the cover flap.

Forse c'è un'infezione.
forsay chay ooneenfetsyonay
You may have an infection.

Ask: Do I need tests?

Devo fare dei controlli?
devoh faray day kontrollee

Prima di tutto deve fare le analisi del sangue.
preemah dee toottoh devay faray lay analeezee del sangway
First you will need a blood test.

Ask: Will it hurt?

Farà male?
farah malay

5 **Say it**

Does he need a blood test?

Where is the children's ward?

Do I need an X-ray?

No, non si preoccupi.
noh, non see prayokkoopee
No, don't worry.

Ask: How long does it take?

Quanto ci vuole?
kwantoh chee vwolay

Ripassa e ripeti
Review and repeat

1 The body

1 **la testa**
lah testah

2 **il braccio**
eel brachoh

3 **il petto**
eel pettoh

4 **lo stomaco**
loh stomakoh

5 **la gamba**
lah gambah

6 **il ginocchio**
eel jeenokkyoh

7 **il piede**
eel pyeday

1 The body

Name the numbered body parts in Italian.

1 head
2 arm
chest 3
4 stomach
leg 5
knee 6
foot 7

2 On the phone

1 **Vorrei parlare con il signor Salvetti.**
vorray parlaray kon eel seennyor salvettee

2 **Sono il dottor Pieri della Bonanni.**
sonoh eel dottor pyayree dellah bonannee

3 **Posso lasciare un messaggio?**
possoh lasharay oon messajjoh?

4 **L'appuntamento è lunedì alle undici.**
lappoontamentoh ay lunedee allay oondeechee

5 **Grazie, arrivederci.**
gratseeay, arreevederchee

2 On the phone

You are arranging an appointment. Follow the conversation, replying in Italian following the English prompts.

Pronto? Tipografia Bartoli.
1 *I'd like to speak to Mr. Salvetti.*

Chi parla, scusi?
2 *It's Dr. Pieri of Bonanni.*

Mi dispiace, il signor Salvetti è in riunione.
3 *Can I leave a message?*

Certo.
4 *The appointment is on Monday at 11 am.*

Benissimo.
5 *Thank you, goodbye.*

3 Clothing

Say the Italian words for the numbered items of clothing.

tie **1**

jacket **2**

pants **3**

4 *skirt*

shoes **5**

pantyhose **6**

3 Clothing

1 **la cravatta**
lah kravattah

2 **la giacca**
lah jakkah

3 **i pantaloni**
ee pantalonee

4 **la gonna**
lah gonnah

5 **le scarpe**
lay skarpay

6 **i collant**
ee kollant

4 At the doctor's

Say these phrases in Italian.

1 *I don't feel well.*

2 *Do I need tests?*

3 *I have a heart condition.*

4 *Do I need to go to the hospital?*

5 *I am pregnant.*

4 At the doctor's

1 **Non mi sento bene.**
non mee sentoh benay

2 **Devo fare dei controlli?**
devoh faray day kontrollee

3 **Ho disturbi cardiaci.**
oh deestoorbee kardeeachee

4 **Devo andare all'ospedale?**
devoh andaray allospedalay

5 **Sono incinta.**
sonoh eencheentah

1 Warm up

Say the months of
the year in Italian.
(pp.28–9)

Ask "Is there an art
gallery?" (pp.48–9)
and "How many
brothers do you
have?" (pp.14–15)

Gli alloggi
At home

The apartment block (**il palazzo**) is the
most common form of urban housing
in Italy. A single-family house (**la
villetta**) is more common in rural areas.
To find out the total number of rooms,
you will need to ask "**Quante stanze?**".
If you want to know how many
bedrooms, ask "**Quante camere?**".

2 Match and repeat

Match the numbered items to the list and test yourself using the flap.

1 **la finestra**
lah feenestrah

2 **il muro**
eel mooroh

3 **il comignolo**
eel comeennyoloh

4 **il tetto**
eel tettoh

5 **la grondaia**
lah grondayah

6 **il viale**
eel veealay

7 **la porta**
lah portah

8 **le persiane**
lay persyanay

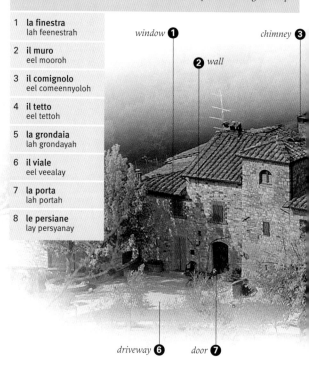

window ❶

❷ *wall*

chimney ❸

driveway ❻   *door* ❼

Cultural tip You almost never see an Italian
home without shutters or roller shades at every window.
These are closed at night and in the heat of the day.
Drapes tend to be more for decoration. Most apartment
blocks have at least one balcony ("il balcone") for each
apartment. These are often filled with plants to make up
for the lack of a garden.

Words to remember

Familiarize yourself with these words and test yourself using the flap.

Quant'è l'affitto al mese?
kwantay laffeettoh al mezay
What is the rent per month?

room	**la stanza** lah stantsah
floor	**il pavimento** eel paveementoh
ceiling	**il soffitto** eel soffeettoh
bedroom	**la camera** lah kamayrah
bathroom	**il bagno** eel bannyoh
kitchen	**la cucina** lah koocheenah
dining room	**la sala da pranzo** lah salah dah prantsoh
living room	**il soggiorno** eel sojjornoh
basement	**la cantina** lah kanteenah
attic	**la soffitta** lah soffeettah

4 *roof*

5 *gutter*

8 *shutters*

Useful phrases

Learn these phrases and test yourself.

C'è il garage?
chay eel garadj

Is there a garage?

È libera subito?
ay leeberah soobeetoh

Is it available soon?

5 Say it

Is there a dining room?

Is it large?

Is it available in July?

L'appartamento è ammobiliato?
lappartamayntoh ay ammobeelyatoh

Is the flat furnished?

1 Warm up

What is the Italian for "table" (pp.20–1), "desk" (pp.80–1), "bed" (pp.60–1), and "restrooms"? (pp.52–3)

How do you say "soft," "beautiful," and "big"? (pp.64–5)

In casa
In the house

If you are renting accommodation in Italy, it is normal to be asked to pay for services such as electricity and heating on top of the rent; for short rentals of vacation flats or villas, they might be included in the rent. You may be asked to pay a security deposit (**versare una caparra** or **cauzione**).

2 Match and repeat

Match the numbered items to the list in the panel on the left. Then test yourself by concealing the Italian with the cover flap.

❶ countertop

1 **il piano di lavoro**
eel peeanoh dee lavoroh

2 **il lavello**
eel lavelloh

3 **il forno a microonde**
eel fornoh ah meekrohonday

4 **il forno**
eel fornoh

5 **il fornello**
eel fornaylloh

6 **il frigorifero**
eel freegoreeferoh

7 **la sedia**
lah sedyah

❺ stove

❹ oven   refrigerator **❻**   **❼** chair

3 In conversation

Questo è il forno.
kwestoh ay eel fornoh

This is the oven.

C'è anche la lavastoviglie?
chay ankay lah lavastoveellyay

Is there a dishwasher, too?

Sì, e il congelatore è grande.
see, ay eel konjelatoray ay granday

Yes, and there's a big freezer.

4 Words to remember

Familiarize yourself with these words and test yourself using the flap.

Il divano è nuovo.
eel deevanoh ay nwovoh
The sofa is new.

microwave **3**

2 sink

wardrobe	**l'armadio** *(m)* larmadeeoh
armchair	**la poltrona** lah poltronah
fireplace	**il caminetto** eel kameenettoh
rug	**il tappeto** eel tappaytoh
bathtub	**la vasca** lah vaskah
toilet	**il bagno** eel banyoh
bathroom sink	**il lavandino** eel lavandeenoh
drapes	**le tende** lay tenday

5 Useful phrases

Learn these phrases and then test yourself using the cover flap to conceal the Italian.

The refrigerator is broken.	**Il frigorifero è rotto.** eel freegoreeferoh ay rottoh
The drapes are ugly.	**Le tende sono brutte.** lay tenday sonoh broottay
Is electricity included?	**La luce è inclusa?** lah loochay ay eenkloosah

6 Say it

Is there a microwave?

I like the fireplace.

What a soft sofa!

Il lavello è nuovo.
eel lavelloh ay nwovoh

The sink is new.

E qui c'è la lavatrice.
ay kwee chay lah lavatreechay

And here's the washing machine.

Che belle piastrelle!
kay bellay piastrellay

What beautiful tiles!

1 Warm up

What is the Italian for "day" and "month"? (pp.28–9)

Say the days of the week. (pp.28–9)

Il giardino
The backyard

The backyard of a house or villa may be communal, or at least partly shared. Check with the rental agent or travel agent. Not a traditional pastime among Italians, gardening for pleasure has become more popular in recent years Garden nurseries stock a wide range of plants.

2 Words to remember

Familiarize yourself with these words and test yourself using the flap.

il tosaerba eel tozaerbah	*lawnmower*
le cesoie lay chezoyay	*shears*
la vanga lah vangah	*spade*
il rastrello eel rastrelloh	*rake*
il vivaio eel veevayoh	*garden nursery*

2 *tree*

3 *soil*

terrace **1**

flowers **7**   *weeds* **8**   **9** *path*

3 Useful phrases

Learn these phrases and then test yourself using the cover flap.

	The gardener comes once a week.	**Il giardiniere viene una volta alla settimana.** eel jardeenyeray vyenay oonah voltah allah setteemanah
	Can you mow the lawn?	**Può tagliare l'erba?** pwoh tallyaray lerbah
	Is the yard private?	**Il giardino è privato?** eel jardeenoh ay preevatoh
	The garden needs watering.	**Bisogna annaffiare il giardino.** beezonnyah annaffyaray eel jardeenoh

4 Match and repeat

Match the numbered items to the words in the panel on the right.

4 *lawn*   **5** *hedge*   **6** *plants*

flowerbed **10**

1 **il patio**
   eel pateeoh

2 **l'albero** *(m)*
   lalberoh

3 **la terra**
   lah terrah

4 **il prato**
   eel pratoh

5 **la siepe**
   lah syepay

6 **le piante**
   lay peeantay

7 **i fiori**
   ee feeoree

8 **le erbacce**
   lay erbacchay

9 **il vialetto**
   eel vyalettoh

10 **l'aiuola** *(f)*
   laywolah

5 Say it

The lawn needs water.

Are there any trees?

The gardener comes on Fridays.

1 Warm up

Say "My name is John." (pp.8–9)

Say "Don't worry." (pp.94–5)

What's "your" in Italian? (pp.12–13)

Gli animali
Pets

If you are considering taking your dog or other pet on an extended trip to Italy, discuss this with your veterinarian well before your departure date, and make sure you have the right documentation and vaccinations. Italy requires an Export Health Certificate.

2 Match and repeat

Match the numbered animals to the Italian words in the panel on the left. Then test yourself using the cover flap.

1 **il gatto**
eel gattoh

2 **il coniglio**
eel koneellyoh

3 **l'uccello** *(m)*
loocchelloh

4 **il pesce**
eel peshay

5 **il cane**
eel kanay

6 **il criceto**
eel kreechetoh

bird ❸

❶ *cat*

❷ *rabbit*

fish ❹

dog ❺

❻ *hamster*

3 Useful phrases

Learn these phrases and then test yourself using the cover flap.

Questo cane è buono? kwestoh kanay ay bwonoh	*Is this dog friendly?*
Posso portare il cane? possoh portaray eel kanay	*Can I bring my dog?*
Ho paura dei gatti. oh paoorah day gattee	*I'm afraid of cats.*
Il mio cane non morde. eel mee-oh kanay non morday	*My dog doesn't bite.*

Questo gatto ha le pulci.
kwestoh gattoh ah lay poolchee
This cat has fleas.

🇮🇹 **Cultural tip** Many dogs in Italy are working dogs, and you may encounter them tethered or roaming free. Approach farms and rural houses with particular care, and keep away from the dog's territory. Look out for warning notices such as "Attenti al cane" (Beware of the dog).

4 Words to remember

Familiarize yourself with these words and test yourself using the flap.

Il mio cane non sta bene.
eel mee-oh kanay non stah benay
My dog is not well.

vet	**il veterinario** eel vetereenareeoh
vaccination	**la vaccinazione** lah vaccheenatsyonay
pet passport	**il pet passport** eel pet passport
dog basket	**la cuccia** lah koocchah
cage	**la gabbia** lah gabbyah
dog bowl	**la ciotola del cane** lah chotolah del kanay
collar	**il collare** eel kollaray
leash	**il guinzaglio** eel gweentsallyoh
fleas	**le pulci** lay poolchee

5 Put into practice

Join in this conversation. Read the Italian on the left and follow the instructions to make your reply. Then test yourself by concealing the answers with the cover flap.

È suo il cane?
ay soo-oh eel kanay
Is this your dog?

Say: *Yes, he's called Sandy.*

Sì, si chiama Sandy.
see, see keeamah sendee

Ho paura dei cani.
oh paoorah day kanee
I'm afraid of dogs.

Say: *Don't worry. He's friendly.*

Non si preoccupi. È buono.
non see preokkoopee. ay bwonoh

Ripassa e ripeti
Review and repeat

Risposte
Answers
Cover with flap

1 Colors

1 **nero**
neroh

2 **azzurra**
azzoorrah

3 **rosso**
rossoh

4 **verde**
verday

5 **gialli**
jallee

1 Colors

Complete the sentences with the Italian for the color in brackets.

1 Questa giacca c'è in ____ ? (black)

2 Prendo la gonna ____ . (blue)

3 Ha questa camicia in ____ ? (red)

4 No, ma c'è in ____ . (green)

5 Ha pantaloni ____ ? (yellow)

2 Kitchen

1 **il fornello**
eel fornaylloh

2 **il frigorifero**
eel freegoreeferoh

3 **il lavello**
eel lavelloh

4 **il forno a microonde**
eel fornoh ah meekrohonday

5 **il forno**
eel fornoh

6 **la sedia**
lah sedyah

2 Kitchen

Say the Italian words for the numbered items.

❶ *stove*

refrigerator ❷

oven ❺

chair ❻

3 House

You are visiting a house in Italy. Join in the conversation, replying in Italian where you see the English prompts.

Questo è il soggiorno.
1 *What a lovely balcony!*

E la cucina è molto bella.
2 *How many bedrooms?*

Ci sono tre camere.
3 *Is there a garage?*

No, ma c'è un giardino molto grande.
4 *Is the house available soon?*

La casa è libera da luglio.
5 *What is the rent per month?*

3 House

1 **Che bel balcone!**
kay bel balkonay

2 **Quante camere ci sono?**
kwantay kameray chee sonoh

3 **C'è il garage?**
chay eel garadj

4 **La casa è libera subito?**
lah kazah ay leeberah soobeetoh

5 **Quant'è l'affitto al mese?**
kwantay laffeettoh al mezay

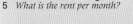

microwave **4**

3 *sink*

4 At home

Say the Italian for the following items.

1 *washing machine*

2 *sofa*

3 *basement*

4 *dining room*

5 *tree*

6 *garden*

4 At home

1 **la lavatrice**
lah lavatreechay

2 **il divano**
eel deevanoh

3 **la cantina**
lah kanteenah

4 **la sala da pranzo**
lah salah dah pranzoh

5 **l'albero**
lalberoh

6 **il giardino**
eel jardeenoh

1 Warm up

Ask "How do I get to the bank?", and "How do I get to the post office?" (pp.50–1 and pp.68–9)

What's the Italian for "passport"? (pp.54–5)

How do you ask "What time is it?" (pp.30–1)

Le poste e la banca
Post office and bank

There aren't as many ATMs in Italy as in the US. But in tourist resorts there is usually a "bureau de change," **il cambio**. In Italy, when withdrawing money or paying with a card, it is common to be asked to enter a PIN number instead of signing.

2 Words to remember: mail

Familiarize yourself with these words and test yourself using the cover flap to conceal the Italian on the left.

la busta lah boostah	*envelope*
il pacco eel pakkoh	*package*
via aerea veeah a-ayreah	*by air mail*
raccomandata rakkomandatah	*registered mail*
i francobolli ee frankobollee	*stamps*
il postino eel posteenoh	*mail carrier*
la cassetta delle lettere lah kassettah dellay letteray	*mailbox*

la cartolina
 lah kartoleenah
 postcard

3 In conversation

Vorrei prelevare dei soldi.
 vorray prelevaray day soldee

I'd like to withdraw some money.

Ha un documento d'identità?
 ah oon dokoomentoh deedenteetah

Do you have any identification?

Sì, ecco il mio passaporto.
 see, ekkoh eel mee-oh passaportoh

Yes, here's my passport.

4 Words to remember: bank

Familiarize yourself with these words and test yourself using the cover flap to conceal the Italian on the right.

la carta di credito
lah kartah dee kredeetoh
credit card

money	**i soldi** ee soldee
traveler's checks	**i travellers cheque** ee traveller chek
teller	**il cassiere** eel kassyeray
notes (bills)	**le banconote** lay bankonotay
ATM	**il bancomat** eel bankomat
PIN	**il pin** eel pin

Come posso pagare?
komay possoh pagaray
How can I pay?

5 Useful phrases

Learn these phrases and then test yourself using the cover flap.

6 Say it

I'd like to change some traveler's checks.

Do I need my passport?

I'd like some stamps.

I'd like to change some money.	**Vorrei cambiare dei soldi.** vorray kambyaray day soldee
What is the exchange rate?	**Quant'è il cambio?** kwantay eel kambyoh
I'd like to withdraw some money.	**Vorrei prelevare dei soldi.** vorray prelevaray day soldee

Può battere il pin.
pwoh battayray eel pin

Please type in your PIN.

Devo anche firmare?
devoh ankay feermaray

Do I need to sign, too?

No, non è necessario.
noh, non ay nechessaryoh

No, that's not necessary.

Riparazioni
Repairs

You can combine the Italian words on these pages with the vocabulary you learned in week 10 to help you explain basic problems and cope with arranging most repairs. When setting up building work or a repair, it's a good idea to agree on the price and method of payment in advance.

2 Words to remember

Familiarize yourself with these words and test yourself using the flap.

l'idraulico leedraooleekoh	*plumber*
l'elettricista lelettreecheestah	*electrician*
il meccanico eel mekkaneekoh	*mechanic*
il muratore eel mooratoray	*handyman*
l'imbianchino leembyankeenoh	*decorator*
il falegname eel falennyamay	*carpenter*
il tecnico eel tayneekoh	*technician*
la donna delle pulizie lah donnah dellay pooleetsyay	*cleaner*

la chiave
lah keeavay
tire iron

Non ho bisogno di un meccanico.
non oh beezonnyoh dee oon mekkaneekoh
I don't need a mechanic.

3 In conversation

La lavatrice non funziona.
lah lavatreechay non foontsyonah

The washing machine is not working.

Sì, il tubo è rotto.
see, eel tooboh ay rottoh

Yes, the hose is broken.

Può ripararlo?
pwoh reepararloh

Can you repair it?

4 Useful phrases

Learn these phrases and then test yourself using the cover flap.

Please clean the bathroom.

Può pulire il bagno?
pwoh pooleeray eel bannyoh

Can you repair the boiler?

Può riparare la caldaia?
pwoh reepararay lah kaldayah

Dove posso farlo riparare?
dovay possoh farloh reepararay
Where can I get this repaired?

Do you know a good electrician?

Conosce un bravo elettricista?
konoshay oon bravoh elettreecheestah

5 Put into practice

Cover up the text on the right and complete the dialogue in Italian.

le piante
lay peeantay
plans

Posso cominciare domani.
possoh komeencharay domanee
I can start tomorrow.

Il suo muretto è rotto.
eel soo-oh mooray-ttoh ay rottoh
Your wall is broken.

Ask: Do you know a good handyman?

Sì, ce n'è uno in paese.
see, chenay oonoh een paesay
Yes, there is one in the village.

Ask: Do you have his phone number?

Conosce un bravo muratore?
konoshay oon bravoh mooratoray

Ha il suo numero di telefono?
ah eel soo-oh noomeroh dee telayfonoh

No, deve cambiarlo.
noh, devay kambeearloh

No, you need to change it.

Può farlo oggi?
pwoh farloh ojjee

Can you do it today?

No, torno domani.
noh, tornoh domanee

No, I'll come back tomorrow.

1 Warm up

Say the days of the week in Italian. (pp.28–9)

How do you say "cleaner"? (pp.110–11)

Say "It's 9:30," "10:45," "12:00." (pp.30–1)

Venire
To come

The verb **venire** (*to come*) is a very common verb that can be used to make a variety of useful idiomatic expressions. Remember that in Italian, the sense of continuing action is implied in the simple present tense— for example, **vengo** can mean both *I come* and *I am coming*.

2 Venire: to come

Say the different forms of **venire** (*to come*) aloud. Use the cover flap to test yourself and, when you are confident, practice the sample sentences below.

(io) vengo (ee-oh) vengoh	*I come*
(tu) vieni (too) vyenee	*you come* *(informal singular)*
(Lei) viene (lay) vyenay	*you come* *(formal singular)*
(lui/lei) viene (loo-ee/lay) vyenay	*he/she/it comes*
(noi) veniamo (noy) veneeamoh	*we come*
(voi) venite (voy) veneetay	*you come* *(plural)*
(loro) vengono (loroh) vengonoh	*they come*
Veniamo tutte le estati. veneeamoh toottay lay estatee	*We come every summer.*
Vengo anch'io. vengoh ankeeoh	*I am coming, too.*
Vengono in treno. vengonoh een trenoh	*They are coming by train.*

Lei viene dalla Nigeria.
lay vyenay dallah neejayreeah
She comes from Nigeria.

■■ Conversational tip Note that when in English you say "come and see" in Italian this translates as "vieni a vedere" (come to see). In the same way, "Shall I come and pick you up?" translated in Italian is "Vengo a prenderti?".

3 Useful phrases

Learn these phrases and then test yourself using the cover flap.

When can I come?	**Quando posso venire?** kwandoh possoh veneeray
Come and see.	**Vieni a vedere.** vyenee ah vederay
The cleaner comes every Monday.	**La donna delle pulizie viene il lunedì.** lah donnah dellay pooleetsyay vyenay eel loonedee

Venite alla mia festa?
veneetay allah mee-ah festah
Are you coming to my party?

Come with me. (informal/formal)	**Vieni/venga con me.** vyenee/vengah kon may

4 Put into practice

Join in this conversation. Read the Italian on the left and follow the instructions to make your reply. Then test yourself by concealing the answers with the cover flap.

Buongiorno. Parrucchiere Leo.
bwonjornoh. parrookkyeray layo
Hello, this is Leo's hair salon.

Say: *I'd like an appointment.*

Vorrei un appuntamento.
vorray oon appoontamentoh

Quando vuol venire?
kwando vwol veneeray
When do you want to come?

Say: *Can I come today?*

Posso venire oggi?
possoh veneeray ojjee

Sì certo, a che ora?
see chertoh, a kay orah
Yes, of course. What time?

Say: *At 10:30.*

Alle dieci e mezzo.
allay deeaychee ay medsoh

1 Warm up

What's the Italian for "big/tall" and "small/short"? (pp.64–5)

Say "The room is big" and "The bed is small." (pp.64–5)

La polizia e il crimine
Police and crime

In an emergency, you can contact the police by dialing 113. You may have to explain your problem in Italian, so some basic vocabulary is useful. In the event of a burglary, the police will usually come to the house.

2 Words to remember: crime

Familiarize yourself with these words.

il furto eel foortoh	*burglary*
il rapporto di polizia eel rapportoh dee poleetseeah	*police report*
il ladro eel ladroh	*thief*
la denuncia lah denoonchah	*statement*
il/la testimone eel/lah testeemonay	*witness*
l'avvocato lavvokatoh	*lawyer*

Voglio un avvocato.
vollyoh oonavvokatoh
I want a lawyer.

3 Useful phrases

Learn these phrases and then test yourself using the cover flap.

Sono stato/a derubato/a. sonoh statoh/ah deroobatoh/ah	*I've been robbed.*
Cosa hanno rubato? kozah annoh roobatoh	*What was stolen?*
Ha visto chi è stato? ah veestoh kee ay statoh	*Did you see who did it?*
Quando è successo? kwandoh ay succhesso	*When did it happen?*

gli oggetti di valore
lly ojjayttee dee valoray
valuables

4 Words to remember: appearance

Learn these words. Remember some adjectives have a feminine form.

Ha i capelli scuri e i baffi.
ah ee kapellee skooree ay ee baffee
He has dark hair and a mustache.

Ha i capelli neri corti.
ah ee kapellee neree kortee
He has short, black hair.

man/men	**l'uomo/gli uomini** lwomoh/lly womeenee
woman/women	**la donna/le donne** lah donnah/lay donnay
tall	**alto/alta** altoh/altah
short	**basso/bassa** bassoh/bassah
young	**giovane** jovanay
old	**vecchio/vecchia** vekkyoh/vekkyah
fat	**grasso/grassa** grassoh/grassah
thin	**magro/magra** magroh/magrah
beard	**la barba** lah barbah
glasses	**gli occhiali** lly okkyalee
long/short hair	**i capelli lunghi/corti** ee kapellee loongee/kortee

Cultural tip If you are affected by a crime or other emergency in Italy, you can go to the Carabinieri, a force that is part of the army and operates even in small towns. Call them by dialing 112.

carabinieri
via Mantellini, 22

5 Put into practice

Practice these phrases. Then use the cover flap to conceal the text on the right and follow the instructions to make your reply in Italian.

Lo può descrivere?
loh pwoh deskreeveray
Can you describe him?

Say: Short and fat.

Basso e grasso.
bassoh ay grassoh

E i capelli?
ay ee kapellee
And the hair?

Say: Long hair and a beard.

Capelli lunghi e barba.
kapellee loongee ay barbah

Ripassa e ripeti
Review and repeat

Risposte
Answers
Cover with flap

1 To come

1 **vengo**
vengoh

2 **viene**
vyenay

3 **veniamo**
veneeamoh

4 **venite**
veneetay

5 **vengono**
vengonoh

1 To come

Fill in the blanks with the correct form of
venire (*to come*).

1 (io) ____ alle quattro.

2 Il giardiniere ____ una volta alla settimana.

3 (noi) ____ in treno.

4 (voi) ____ con noi?

5 I miei genitori ____ lunedì.

2 Bank and post

1 **le banconote**
lay bankonotay

2 **la carta di credito**
lah cartah dee kredeetoh

3 **il pacco**
eel pakkoh

4 **i francobolli**
ee frankobollee

5 **la cartolina**
lah kartoleenah

2 Bank and post office

Name the numbered
items in Italian.

credit card ❷

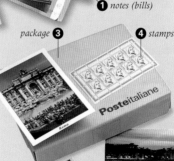

❶ notes (bills)

package ❸

❹ stamps

❺ postcard

Risposte
Answers
Cover with flap

3 Appearance

What do these descriptions mean?

1 **Un uomo alto e magro.**

2 **Una donna con i capelli corti e gli occhiali.**

3 **Sono bassa e ho i capelli lunghi.**

4 **È vecchia e grassa.**

5 **Lui ha gli occhi azzurri e la barba.**

3 Appearance

1 *A tall, thin man.*

2 *A woman with short hair and glasses.*

3 *I'm short and I have long hair.*

4 *She is old and fat.*

5 *He has blue eyes and a beard.*

4 The pharmacy

You are asking a pharmacist for advice. Join in the conversation, replying in Italian where you see the English prompts.

Buongiorno, dica?
1 *I have a cough.*

Ha anche il raffreddore?
2 *No, but I have a headache.*

Prenda queste pastiglie.
3 *Do you have that as a syrup?*

Certo. Ecco lo sciroppo.
4 *Thank you. How much is that?*

Nove euro.
5 *Here you are. Goodbye.*

4 The pharmacy

1 **Ho la tosse.**
oh lah tossay

2 **No, ma ho mal di testa.**
noh, mah oh mal dee testah

3 **Le ha in sciroppo?**
lay ah een sheeroppoh

4 **Grazie. Quant'è?**
gratseeay.
kwantay

5 **Ecco. Arrivederci.**
ekkoh.
arreevederchee

1 Warm up

What is the Italian for "museum" and "art gallery"? (pp.48–9)

Say "What beautiful curtains!" (pp.100–1)

Ask "Do you want…?" informally. (p.22–3)

Il tempo libero
Leisure time

Italy, with its long history and rich culture, provides numerous opportunities for cultural pursuits, as well as modern leisure activities. Many Italians are interested in the arts and spend the weekends in historic cities (**città d'arte**) or, when the weather is warm, at the seaside.

2 Words to remember

Familiarize yourself with these words and test yourself using the cover flap to conceal the Italian on the left.

il teatro eel tayatroh	*theater*
il cinema eel cheenemah	*movie theater*
la discoteca lah diskotekah	*discotheque*
la musica lah moozeekah	*music*
l'arte *(f)* lartay	*art*
lo sport loh sport	*sports*
viaggiare veeajjaray	*traveling*
i videogiochi ee veedayohjokkee	*video games*

Amo l'opera.
amoh lopayrah
I love opera.

gli spettatori
lly spettatoree
audience

3 In conversation

Vuoi giocare a tennis?
vwoee jokaray ah tennees

Do you want to play tennis?

No, lo sport non mi piace.
noh. loh sport non mee peeachay

No, I don't like sports.

Cosa fai nel tempo libero?
kozah faee nel tempoh leeberoh

What do you do in your free time?

4 Useful phrases

Learn these phrases and then test yourself using the cover flap.

Detesto i videogiochi.
detestoh ee
veedayohjokkee
I hate video games.

la galleria
lah galereeah
balcony

la platea
lah platayah
orchestra

What do you do (formal/informal) in your spare time?	**Cosa fa/fai nel tempo libero?** kozah fah/faee nel tempoh leeberoh
I like the theater.	**Mi piace il teatro.** mee peeachay eel teatroh
I prefer the movies.	**Io preferisco il cinema.** ee-oh preferisko eel cheenemah
I'm interested in art.	**Mi interessa l'arte.** mee eenteressah lartay
That's boring!	**Che noia!** kay noeeah

5 Say it

I'm interested in music.

I prefer sports.

I don't like opera.

Mi piace lo shopping.
mee peeachay loh
shoppeen

I like shopping.

Detesto lo shopping.
Detestoh loh shoppeen

I hate shopping.

Non c'è problema, vado da sola.
non chay problemah,
vadoh dah solah

No problem, I'll go on my own.

1 Warm up

Ask "Do you (formal) want to play tennis?" (pp.22–3, pp.118–19)

Say "I like the theater" and "I prefer traveling." (pp.118–19)

Say "That doesn't interest me." (pp.118–19)

Lo sport e gli hobby
Sports and hobbies

The verb **fare** (*to do*) is useful for talking about hobbies. With sports you can also use **giocare** (*to play*)—for example, **gioco a tennis** (*I play tennis*). **Fare** is also used to describe the weather, as in **fa freddo** (*it's cold*).

2 Words to remember

Memorize these words and then test yourself.

il calcio eel kalchoh	*soccer*
il rugby eel regbee	*rugby*
il tennis eel tennees	*tennis*
il nuoto eel nwotoh	*swimming*
la vela lah velah	*sailing*
la pesca lah peskah	*fishing*
la pittura lah peettoorah	*painting*
la palestra lah palestrah	*gymnastics*

il bunker
eel bunker
bunker

il golfista
eel golfeestah
golfer

Gioco a golf tutti i giorni.
jokoh ah golf toottee ee jornee
I play golf every day.

3 Useful phrases

Familiarize yourself with these phrases.

Gioco a rugby. jokoh ah regbee	*I play rugby.*
Gioca a tennis. jokah ah tennees	*He plays tennis.*
Fa un corso di pittura. fah oon korsoh dee peettoorah	*She is on a painting course.*

4 Fare: to do or to make

The verb **fare** (*to do* or *to make*) is also used to describe the weather. Learn its different forms and practice the sample sentences below.

I do	**(io) faccio** (ee-oh) facchoh
you do (informal singular)	**(tu) fai** (too) faee
you do (formal singular)	**(Lei) fa** (lay) fah
he/she/it does	**(lui/lei) fa** (loo-ee/lay) fah
we do	**(noi) facciamo** (noy) facchamoh
you do (plural)	**(voi) fate** (voy) fatay
they do	**(loro) fanno** (loroh) fannoh
What do you do? (formal/informal)	**Cosa fai/fate?** kozah faee/fatay
I go hiking.	**Faccio escursionismo.** facchoh ayskursyoneesmoh

Fa caldo oggi.
fah kaldoh ojjee
It's hot today.

la bandierina
lah
bandeeayreenah
flag

il campo da golf
eel kampoh dah
golf
golf course

5 Put into practice

Learn these phrases. Then cover up the text on the right and complete the dialogue in Italian. Check your answers.

Cosa ti piace fare?
kozah tee peeachay
faray
What do you like doing?

Say: I like playing tennis.

Mi piace giocare a tennis.
mee peeachay jokaray
ah tennees

Giochi anche a calcio?
jokee anchay ah
kalchoh
Do you play football as well?

Say: No. I play rugby.

No. Gioco a rugby.
noh. jokoh ah regbee

Quando giochi?
kwandoh jokee
When do you play?

Say: I play every week.

Gioco tutte le settimane.
jokoh toottay lay
setteemanay

1 Warm up

Say "my husband"
and "my wife."
(pp.12–13)

How do you say
"lunch" and "dinner"
in Italian? (pp.20–1)

Say "Sorry, I'm busy."
(pp.32–3)

Rapporti sociali
Socializing

The Italian dinner table is the center
of the social world; you can expect to
do a lot of socializing while enjoying
food and wine. It is best to use the
more polite **Lei** form at first to talk
to people you meet socially; when
they start to call you **tu**, you can
reciprocate.

2 Useful phrases

Learn these phrases and then test yourself.

Vuol venire a cena con me? vwol veneeray ah chenah con may	*Would you like to come to dinner with me?*
È libero/a mercoledì prossimo? ay leeberoh/ah merkoledee prosseemoh	*Are you free next Wednesday?*
Magari un'altra volta. magaree oonaltrah voltah	*Perhaps another time.*

▯▯ Cultural tip When you go to someone's
house for the first time, it is polite to bring flowers,
chocolate, or a bottle of good wine. If you are invited
again, having seen your host's house, you can bring
something a little more personal.

3 In conversation

Vuol venire a cena da me martedì?
vwol veneeray ah chenah dah may martedee

Would you like to come to dinner on Tuesday?

Mi dispiace, martedì non posso.
mee deespeeachay, martedee non possoh

I'm sorry, I can't on Tuesday.

Facciamo giovedì?
facchamoh jovedee

What about Thursday?

4 Words to remember

Familiarize yourself with these words and test yourself using the flap.

la padrona di casa
lah padronah dee kazah
hostess

l'ospite
lospeetay
guest

party	**la festa** lah festah
dinner party	**la cena** lah chenah
invitation	**l'invito** *(m)* leenveetoh
reception	**il rinfresco** eel reenfreskoh
gift	**il regalo** eel regaloh

5 Put into practice

Join in this conversation.

Facciamo una festa sabato. Siete liberi? facchamoh oonah festah sabatoh. seeaytay leeberee *We're having a party on Saturday. Are you free?* *Say: Yes, how nice!*	**Sì, che bello!** see, kay belloh
Benissimo. beneesseemoh *That's great.* *Ask: What time does it start?*	**A che ora comincia?** ah kay orah komeenchah

Grazie dell'invito.
gratseeay delleenveetoh
Thank you for inviting us.

Benissimo.
beneesseemoh

That's great.

Porti suo marito.
portee soo-oh mareetoh

Please bring your husband.

Grazie. A che ora?
gratseeay. ah kay orah

Thank you. What time?

Ripassa e ripeti
Review and repeat

1 Animals

1 **il pesce**
eel peshay

2 **l'uccello**
loocchelloh

3 **il coniglio**
eel koneellyoh

4 **il gatto**
eel gattoh

5 **il criceto**
eel kreechetoh

6 **il cane**
eel kanay

1 Animals

Name the numbered animals in Italian.

bird **2**

fish **1**

hamster **5**

cat **4**

2 I like...

1 **Mi piace il rugby.**
mee peeachay eel regbee

2 **Non mi piace il golf.**
non mee peeachay eel golf

3 **Mi piace la pittura.**
mee peeachay lah peettoorah

2 I like...

Say the following in Italian:

1 *I like rugby.*

2 *I don't like golf.*

3 *I like to paint.*

3 rabbit

6 dog

Risposte
Answers
Cover with flap

3 To do

Use the correct form of the verb **fare** (*to do*) in these sentences.

1 Tu _____ vela?

2 Lei _____ un corso di pittura.

3 Cosa le piace _____ ?

4 _____ freddo oggi.

5 Voi _____ palestra?

6 Io _____ nuoto.

3 To do

1 **fai**
faee

2 **fa**
fah

3 **fare**
faray

4 **fa**
fah

5 **fate**
fatay

6 **faccio**
facchoh

4 An invitation

You are invited for lunch. Join in the conversation, replying in Italian following the English prompts.

Vuol venire a pranzo da me sabato?
1 *I'm sorry, I can't on Saturday.*

Facciamo domenica?
2 *Great. I'm free on Sunday.*

Porti i bambini.
3 *Thank you. What time?*

All'una.
4 *See you on Sunday.*

4 An invitation

1 **Mi dispiace, sabato non posso.**
mee deespeeachay, sabatoh non possoh

2 **Benissimo. Sono libera domenica.**
beneesseemoh. sonoh leeberah domeneekah

3 **Grazie. A che ora?**
gratseeay. ah kay orah

4 **Arrivederci a domenica.**
arreevederchee ah domeneekah

Reinforce and progress

Regular practice is the key to maintaining and advancing your language skills. In this section you will find a variety of suggestions for reinforcing and extending your knowledge of Italian. Many involve returning to exercises in the book and using the dictionaries to extend their scope. Go back through the lessons in a different order, mix and match activities to make up your own 15-minute daily program, or focus on topics that are of particular relevance to your current needs.

Keep warmed up
Revisit the Warm Up boxes to remind yourself of key words and phrases. Make sure you work your way through all of them on a regular basis.

1 Warm up

How do you say "I'm sorry"? (pp.32–3)

Say "I'd like an appointment." (pp.32–3)

How do you say "with whom?" in Italian? (pp.32–3)

2 I'd like...

Say "I'd like" the following:

❶ sugar   croissant ❶

cappuccino ❸

❶ black coffee

Review and repeat again
Work through a Review and Repeat lesson as a way of reinforcing words and phrases presented in the course. Return to the main lesson for any topic on which you are no longer confident.

3 In conversation: taxi

Carry on conversing
Reread the In Conversation panels. Say both parts of the conversation, paying attention to the pronunciation. Where possible, try incorporating new words from the dictionary.

Al mercato di San Lorenzo, per favore.
al merkatoh dee san lorentsoh, per favoray

To the San Lorenzo market, please.

Benissimo, signore.
beneesseemoh, seennyoray

Very well, sir.

Mi lasci qui, per favore.
mee lashee kwee, per favoray

Can you drop me please?

4 Useful phrases

Learn these phrases and then test yourself using the cover flap.

What time do you open/close?	A che ora aprite/chiudete?	ah kay orah apreetay/keeoodetay
Where are the restrooms?	Dov'è la toilette?	dovay lahtoyeeletay
Is there disabled access?	C'è l'accesso per i disabili?	chay lacchayssoh per ee deesabeelee

Practice phrases
Return to the Useful Phrases and Put into Practice exercises. Test yourself using the cover flap. When you are confident, devise your own versions of the phrases, using new words from the dictionary.

Match, repeat, and extend

Remind yourself of words related to specific topics by returning to the Match and Repeat and Words to Remember exercises. Test yourself using the cover flap. Discover new words in that area by referring to the dictionary and menu guide.

Match and repeat

Match the numbered items in this scene with the text in the panel.

il finocchio
eel feenokkeeoh

il cavolfiore
eel kavolfeeoray

la lattuga
lah lattoogah

i peperoni
ee paypaironee

le patate
lay patatay

l'aglio *(m)*
lallyoh

i pomodori
ee pomodoree

gli asparagi
lly asparajee

❶ fennel
❷ cauliflower
❸ lettuce
❹ peppers
❺ potatoes
❻ garlic
❼ tomatoes
❽ asparagus

Say it again

The Say It exercises are a useful instant reminder for each lesson. Practice these, using your own vocabulary variations from the dictionary or elsewhere in the lesson.

6 Say it

The lawn needs water.

Are there any trees?

The gardener comes on Fridays.

Using other resources

In addition to working with this book, try the following language extension ideas:

- Visit Italy and try out your new skills with native speakers. Or find out if there is an Italian community near you. There may be shops, cafés, restaurants, and clubs. Try to visit some of these and use your Italian to order food and drink and strike up conversations. Most native speakers will be happy to speak Italian to you.

- Join a language class or club. There are usually evening and day classes available at a variety of different levels. Or you could start a club yourself if you have friends who are also interested in keeping up their Italian.

- Look at Italian magazines and newspapers. The pictures will help you to understand the text. Advertisements are also a useful way of expanding your vocabulary.

- Use the Internet, where you can find all kinds of websites for learning languages, some of which offer free online help and activities. You can also find Italian websites for anything from renting a house to shampooing your pet. You can even access Italian radio and TV stations online. Start by going to an Italian search engine, such as *iltrovatore.it*, and typing in a hobby or sport that interests you, or set yourself a challenge, such as finding a two-bedroom apartment for rent in Florence.

Menu guide

This guide lists the most common terms you may encounter on Italian menus or when shopping for food. If you can't find an exact phrase, try looking up its component parts.

A

abbacchio alla romana *Roman-style spring lamb*
acciughe sott'olio *anchovies in oil*
aceto *vinegar*
acqua *water*
acqua minerale gassata *sparkling mineral water*
acqua minerale non gassata *still mineral water*
acqua naturale *still mineral water, tap water*
affettato misto *variety of cold, sliced meats*
affogato al caffè *hot espresso on ice cream*
aglio *garlic*
agnello *lamb*
albicocche *apricots*
al forno *roast*
amatriciana *chopped bacon and tomato sauce*
ananas *pineapple*
anatra *duck*
anatra all'arancia *duck in orange sauce*
anguilla in umido *stewed eel*
anguria *watermelon*
antipasti *appetizers*
antipasti misti *mixed appetizers*
aperitivo *aperitif*
aragosta *lobster*
arancia *orange*
aranciata *orangeade*
aringa *herring*
arista di maiale al forno *roast chine of pork*
arrosto *roast*
arrosto di tacchino *roast turkey*
asparagi *asparagus*
avocado all'agro *avocado with dressing*

B

baccalà *dried cod*
baccalà alla vicentina *Vicentine-style dried cod*
bagnacauda *vegetables (often raw) in a sauce of oil, garlic, and anchovy*
Barbaresco *dry red wine from Piedmont*

Barbera *dry red wine from Piedmont*
Bardolino *dry red wine from the Veneto region*
Barolo *dark, dry red wine from Piedmont*
basilico *basil*
bavarese *ice-cream cake with cream*
bel paese *soft, white cheese*
besciamella *white sauce*
bignè *cream puff*
birra *beer*
birra chiara *light beer, lager*
birra grande *large beer*
birra piccola *small beer*
birra scura *dark beer*
bistecca ai ferri *grilled steak*
bistecca (di manzo) *steak*
bolognese *ground beef and tomato sauce*
braciola di maiale *pork steak*
branzino al forno *baked sea bass*
brasato *braised beef with herbs*
bresaola *dried, salted beef eaten with oil and lemon*
brioche *type of croissant*
brodo *clear broth*
brodo di pollo *chicken broth*
brodo vegetale *clear vegetable broth*
budino *pudding*
burro *butter*
burro di acciughe *anchovy butter*

C

caciotta *tender, white cheese from Central Italy*
caffè *coffee*
caffè corretto *espresso with a dash of liqueur*
caffè latte *half coffee, half hot milk*
caffè lungo *weak espresso*
caffè macchiato *espresso with a dash of milk*
caffè ristretto *strong espresso*
calamari in umido *stewed squid*

calamaro *squid*
calzone *folded pizza with tomato and cheese*
camomilla *chamomile tea*
cannella *cinnamon*
cannelloni al forno *baked egg pasta rolls stuffed with meat*
cappuccino *espresso with foaming milk sprinkled with cocoa powder*
capretto al forno *roast kid*
carbonara *sauce of egg, bacon, and cheese*
carciofi *artichokes*
carciofini sott'olio *baby artichokes in oil*
carne *meat*
carote *carrots*
carpaccio *finely sliced beef fillets with oil, lemon, and parmesan*
carré di maiale al forno *roast pork loin*
cassata siciliana *ice-cream cake with chocolate, glacé fruit, and ricotta*
castagne *chestnuts*
cavoletti di Bruxelles *Brussels sprouts*
cavolfiore *cauliflower*
cavolo *cabbage*
cefalo *mullet*
cernia *grouper (fish)*
charlotte *ice-cream cake with cream, cookies, and fruit*
Chianti *dark red Tuscan wine*
cicoria *chicory*
cicorino *small chicory plants*
ciliege *cherries*
cime di rapa *sprouting broccoli*
cioccolata *chocolate*
cioccolata calda *hot chocolate*
cipolle *onions*
cocktail di gamberetti *shrimp cocktail*
conchiglie alla marchigiana *pasta shells in tomato sauce with ham, celery, carrot, and parsley*
coniglio *rabbit*
coniglio in umido *stewed rabbit*
consommé *clear meat or chicken broth*

contorni *vegetables*
coperto *cover charge*
coppa *cured neck of pork*
costata alla fiorentina *T-bone veal steak*
costata di manzo *T-bone beef steak*
cotechino *spiced pork sausage for boiling*
cotoletta *veal, pork, or lamb chop*
cotoletta ai ferri *grilled veal or pork chop*
cotoletta alla milanese *veal chop in breadcrumbs*
cotoletta alla valdostana *veal chop with ham and cheese, in breadcrumbs*
cotolette di agnello *lamb chops*
cotolette di maiale *pork chops*
cozze *mussels*
cozze alla marinara *mussels in white wine*
crema *custard dessert made with eggs and milk*
crema al caffè *coffee custard dessert*
crema al cioccolato *chocolate custard dessert*
crema di funghi *cream of mushroom soup*
crema di piselli *cream of pea soup*
crema pasticciera *confectioner's custard*
crêpes Suzette *crepes flambéed with orange sauce*
crescente *fried bread made with flour, lard, and eggs*
crespelle *savory crepe*
crostata di frutta *fruit tart*

D, E

dadi *bouillon cubes*
datteri *dates*
degustazione *tasting*
degustazione di vini *wine tasting*
dentice al forno *baked dentex (type of sea bream)*
digestivo *dessert liqueur*
dolci *sweets, desserts, cakes*
endivia belga *white chicory*
entrecôte (di manzo) *beef entrecote*
espresso *strong, black coffee*

F

fagiano *pheasant*
fagioli *beans*
fagioli borlotti in umido *borlotti (kidney beans)*

in sauce of tomato, vegetables, and herbs
fagiolini *long, green beans*
faraona *guinea fowl*
fegato *liver*
fegato alla veneta *liver in butter with onions*
fegato con salvia e burro *liver in butter and sage*
fettuccine *ribbon-shaped pasta*
fichi *figs*
filetti di pesce persico *fillets of perch*
filetti di sogliola *fillets of sole*
filetto ai ferri *grilled fillet of beef*
filetto al cognac *fillet of beef flambé*
filetto al pepe verde *fillet of beef with green peppercorns*
filetto al sangue *rare fillet of beef*
filetto ben cotto *well-done fillet of beef*
filetto (di manzo) *fillet of beef*
filetto medio *medium-cooked fillet of beef*
finocchi gratinati *fennel au gratin*
finocchio *fennel*
fonduta *cheese fondue*
formaggi misti *variety of cheeses*
fragole *strawberries*
fragole con gelato/panna *strawberries and ice cream/cream*
frappé *fruit or milk shake with crushed ice*
Frascati *dry white wine from area around Rome*
frittata *type of omelet*
frittata alle erbe *herb omelet*
fritto misto *mixed seafood in batter*
frittura di pesce *variety of fried fish*
frutta *fruit*
frutta alla fiamma *fruit flambé*
frutta secca *dried nuts and raisins*
frutti di bosco *mixture of strawberries, raspberries, mulberries, etc.*
frutti di mare *seafood*
funghi *mushrooms*
funghi trifolati *mushrooms fried in garlic and parsley*

G

gamberetti *shrimp*
gamberi *large shrimp*
gamberoni *jumbo shrimp*

gazzosa *clear lemonade*
gelatina *gelatin*
gelato *ice cream*
gelato di crema *vanilla-flavored ice cream*
gelato di frutta *fruit-flavored ice cream*
gnocchetti verdi agli spinaci e al gorgonzola *small flour, potato, and spinach dumplings with melted gorgonzola*
gnocchi *small flour and potato dumplings*
gnocchi alla romana *small milk and semolina dumplings with butter*
Gorgonzola *strong blue cheese from Lombardy*
grancevola *spiny spider crab*
granchio *crab*
granita *crushed ice drink*
grigliata di pesce *grilled fish*
grigliata mista *mixed grill (meat or fish)*
grissini *thin, crisp breadsticks*
gruviera *Gruyère cheese*

I

indivia *endive*
insalata *salad*
insalata caprese *salad of tomatoes and mozzarella*
insalata di funghi porcini *boletus mushroom salad*
insalata di mare *seafood salad*
insalata di nervetti *boiled beef or veal served cold with beans and pickles*
insalata di pomodori *tomato salad*
insalata di riso *rice salad*
insalata mista *mixed salad*
insalata russa *Russian salad (diced cooked vegetables in mayonnaise)*
insalata verde *green salad*
involtini *meat rolls stuffed with ham and herbs*

L

lamponi *raspberries*
lasagne al forno *meat lasagna with cheese*
latte *milk*
latte macchiato con cioccolato *hot milk sprinkled with cocoa*
lattuga *lettuce*
leggero *light*
legumi *legumes (beans)*
lemonsoda *sparkling lemon drink*
lenticchie *lentils*
lepre *hare*

limonata *lemon-flavored soda*
limone *lemon*
lingua *tongue*

M

macedonia di frutta *fruit salad*
maiale *pork*
maionese *mayonnaise*
mandarino *mandarin*
mandorla *almond*
manzo *beef*
marroni *chestnuts*
Marsala *fortified wine*
marzapane *marzipan*
mascarpone *soft, mild cheese*
medaglioni di vitello *veal medallions*
mela *apple*
melanzane *eggplant*
melone *melon*
menta *mint*
meringata *meringue pie*
merluzzo *cod*
merluzzo alla pizzaiola *cod in tomato sauce with anchovies and capers*
merluzzo in bianco *cod with oil and lemon*
messicani in gelatina *rolls of veal in gelatin*
millefoglie *pastry layered with custard*
minestra in brodo *noodle soup*
minestrone *vegetable soup with rice or pasta*
mirtilli *bilberries*
more *mulberries or blackberries*
moscato *sweet wine*
mousse al cioccolato *chocolate mousse*
mozzarella *buffalo cheese*
mozzarella in carrozza *fried slices of bread and mozzarella*

N, O

nasello *hake*
nocciole *hazelnuts*
noce moscata *nutmeg*
noci *walnuts*
nodino *veal chop*
olio *oil*
origano *oregano*
osso buco *stewed shin of veal*
ostriche *oysters*

P

paglia e fieno *mixed plain and green tagliatelle*
paillard di manzo *slices of grilled beef*
paillard di vitello *slices of grilled veal*
pane *bread*
panino *filled roll*
panna *cream*
parmigiana di melanzane *eggplant baked with cheese*
pasta al forno *pasta baked in white sauce and grated cheese*
pasta e fagioli *thick soup with puréed borlotti beans and pasta rings*
pasta e piselli *pasta with peas*
pasticcio di fegato d'oca *baked pasta dish with goose liver*
pasticcio di lepre *baked pasta dish with hare*
pasticcio di maccheroni *baked macaroni*
pastina in brodo *noodle soup*
patate *potatoes*
patate al forno/arrosto *roast potatoes*
patate fritte *french fries*
patate in insalata *potato salad*
pecorino *strong, hard sheep's milk cheese*
penne *pasta quills*
penne ai quattro formaggi *pasta with four-cheese sauce*
penne all'arrabbiata *pasta with tomato and chili pepper sauce*
penne panna e prosciutto *pasta with cream and ham sauce*
pepe *pepper (spice)*
peperoncino *crushed chili pepper*
peperoni *peppers*
peperoni ripieni *stuffed peppers*
peperoni sott'olio *peppers in oil*
pera *pear*
pesca *peach*
pesce *fish*
pesce al cartoccio *fish baked in foil with herbs*
pesce in carpione *marinaded fish*
pesto *sauce of basil, pine nuts, Parmesan, garlic, and oil*
pinot *dry white wine from the Veneto region*
pinzimonio *raw vegetables with oil and vinegar*
piselli *peas*
piselli al prosciutto *broth with peas, ham, and basil*
pizzaiola *slices of cooked beef in tomato sauce, oregano, and anchovies*

pizzoccheri alla Valtellinese *pasta strips with vegetables and cheese*
polenta *boiled cornmeal left to set and sliced*
polenta e osei *polenta with small birds*
polenta pasticciata *layers of polenta, tomato sauce, and cheese*
pollo *chicken*
pollo alla cacciatora *chicken in white wine and mushroom sauce*
pollo alla diavola *deep-fried chicken pieces*
polpette *meatballs*
polpettone *meatloaf*
pomodori *tomatoes*
pomodori ripieni *stuffed tomatoes*
pompelmo *grapefruit*
porri *leeks*
prezzemolo *parsley*
primi piatti *first courses*
prosciutto cotto *cooked ham*
prosciutto crudo *type of cured ham*
prugne *plums*
punte di asparagi all'agro *asparagus tips in oil and lemon*
purè di patate *mashed potatoes*
puttanesca *tomato sauce with anchovies, capers, and black olives*

Q, R

quaglie *quails*
radicchio *chicory*
ragù *meat-based sauce*
rapanelli *radishes*
ravioli *stuffed pasta parcels*
ravioli al pomodoro *meat ravioli in tomato sauce*
razza *skate*
ricotta *ricotta cheese*
risi e bisi *risotto with peas and ham*
riso *rice*
risotto *rice cooked in stock*
risotto alla castellana *risotto with mushroom, ham, cream, and cheese*
risotto alla milanese *risotto with saffron*
risotto al nero di seppia *risotto with cuttlefish ink*
risotto al tartufo *truffle risotto*
roast-beef all'inglese *thinly sliced cold roast beef*
robiola *type of soft cheese from Lombardy*
rognone trifolato *kidney in garlic, oil, and parsley*
rosatello/rosato *rosé wine*
rosmarino *rosemary*

S

salame *salami*
sale *salt*
salmone affumicato *smoked salmon*
salsa cocktail/rosa *mayonnaise and ketchup sauce for fish and seafood*
salsa di pomodoro *tomato sauce*
salsa tartara *tartar sauce*
salsa vellutata *white sauce made with clear broth instead of milk*
salsa verde *sauce for meat, with parsley and oil*
salsiccia *sausage*
salsiccia di cinghiale *wild boar sausage*
salsiccia di maiale *pork sausage*
saltimbocca alla romana *slices of veal stuffed with ham and sage and fried*
salvia *sage*
sambuca (con la mosca) *aniseed-flavor liqueur served with a coffee bean*
sarde ai ferri *grilled sardines*
scaloppine *veal escalopes*
scaloppine al prezzemolo *veal escalopes with parsley*
scamorza alla griglia *grilled soft cheese*
scampi alla griglia *grilled shrimp*
secco *dry*
secondi piatti *second courses, main courses*
sedano *celery*
selvaggina *game*
semifreddo *dessert of ice cream and sponge cakes*
senape *mustard*
seppie in umido *stewed cuttlefish*
servizio compreso *service charge included*
servizio escluso *service charge excluded*
Soave *dry white wine from the Veneto region*
sogliola *sole*
sogliola ai ferri *grilled sole*
sogliola al burro *sole cooked in butter*
sogliola alla mugnaia *sole cooked in flour and butter*
sorbetto *sorbet, soft ice cream*
soufflé al formaggio *cheese soufflé*
soufflé al prosciutto *ham soufflé*
speck *cured, smoked ham*
spezzatino di vitello *veal stew*

spiedini *assorted chunks of spit-cooked meat or fish*
spinaci *spinach*
spinaci all'agro *spinach with oil and lemon*
spremuta di ... *freshly squeezed ... juice*
spumante *sparkling wine*
stracchino *soft cheese from Lombardy*
stracciatella *soup of beaten eggs in clear broth*
strudel di mele *apple strudel*
succo di ... ... *juice*
sugo al tonno *tomato sauce with garlic, tuna, and parsley*

T

tacchino ripieno *stuffed turkey*
tagliata *finely cut beef fillet cooked in the oven*
tagliatelle *thin pasta strips*
tagliatelle rosse *tagliatelle with chopped red peppers*
tagliatelle verdi *tagliatelle with spinach*
tagliolini *thin soup noodles*
tartine *small sandwiches*
tartufo *ice cream covered in cocoa or chocolate; truffle*
tè *tea*
tiramisù *dessert with coffee-soaked sponge, Marsala, mascarpone, and cocoa powder*
tonno *tuna*
torta *tart, flan*
torta di ricotta *type of cheesecake*
torta salata *savory quiche*
tortellini *pasta shapes filled with minced pork, ham, Parmesan, and nutmeg*
trancio di palombo *smooth dogfish steak*
trancio di pesce spada *swordfish steak*
trenette col pesto *flat spaghetti with pesto sauce*
triglie *mullet (fish)*
trippa *tripe*
trota *trout*
trota affumicata *smoked trout*
trota al burro *trout cooked in butter*
trota alle mandorle *trout with almonds*
trota bollita *boiled trout*

U

uccelletti *small birds wrapped in bacon, served on cocktail sticks*
uova *eggs*

uova alla coque *boiled eggs*
uova al tegamino con pancetta *fried eggs and bacon*
uova farcite *eggs with tuna, capers, and mayonnaise filling*
uova sode *hard-boiled eggs*
uva *grapes*
uva bianca *white grapes*
uva nera *black grapes*

V

vellutata di asparagi *creamed asparagus with egg yolks*
vellutata di piselli *creamed peas with egg yolks*
verdura *vegetables*
vermicelli *very fine, thin pasta, often used in soups*
vino *wine*
vino bianco *white wine*
vino da dessert *dessert wine*
vino da pasto *table wine*
vino da tavola *table wine*
vino rosso *red wine*
vitello *veal*
vitello tonnato *cold sliced veal in tuna, anchovy, oil, and lemon sauce*
vongole *clams*

W, Z

würstel *hot dog*
zabaglione *creamy dessert of eggs, sugar, and Marsala*
zafferano *saffron*
zucca *pumpkin*
zucchine *zucchini*
zucchine al pomodoro *zucchini in tomato, garlic, and parsley sauce*
zucchine ripiene *stuffed zucchini*
zuccotto *ice-cream cake with sponge cake, cream, and chocolate*
zuppa *soup*
zuppa di cipolle *onion soup*
zuppa di cozze *mussel soup*
zuppa di lenticchie *lentil soup*
zuppa di pesce *fish soup*
zuppa di verdura *vegetable soup*
zuppa inglese *sponge cake with fruit, custard, and whipped cream*

Dictionary
English to Italian

The gender of an Italian noun is indicated by the word for *the*: **il** or **lo** (masculine), **la** (feminine), and their plural forms **i** or **gli** (masculine) and **le** (feminine). When **lo** or **la** are abbreviated to **l'** in front of a vowel or "h", then the gender is indicated by the abbreviations "(m)" or "(f)." Italian adjectives "(adj)" vary according to the gender and number of the word they describe, and the masculine form is shown here. In general, adjectives that end in **-o** adopt an **-a** ending in the feminine form, and those that end in **-e** usually stay the same. Plural endings are **-i** for masculine and **-e** for feminine.

A

a un/uno/una/un'
about: about 16 circa 16; *a book about Venice* un libro su Venezia
accelerator l'acceleratore (m)
accident l'incidente (m)
accommodation l'alloggio (m), il posto
accountant il ragioniere/la ragioniera
ache il dolore
adapter il riduttore
address l'indirizzo (m)
admission charge il prezzo d'ingresso
advance (on payment) il anticipo; *in advance* anticipato
after dopo
afternoon il pomeriggio
aftershave il dopobarba
again di nuovo
against contro
agenda l'ordine del giorno (m)
AIDS l'Aids (f)
air l'aria (f)
air conditioning l'aria condizionata (f)
aircraft l'aereo (m)
airline la linea aerea
air mail via aerea
air mattress il materassino gonfiabile
airport l'aeroporto (m)
airport bus l'autobus navetta (m)
aisle (in supermarket, etc.) la fila
alarm clock la sveglia
alcohol l'alcol (m)
all tutto; *all the streets* tutte le strade; *that's all* questo è tutto

allergic allergico
allowed permesso
almost quasi
alone solo
Alps le Alpi
already già
always sempre
am: I am (io) sono
ambulance l'ambulanza (f)
America l'America (f)
American americano
and e
ankle la caviglia
anniversary il anniversario
another un altro, un'altra
answering machine la segreteria telefonica
antique shop l'antiquario (m)
antiseptic l'antisettico (m)
apartment l'appartamento (m)
aperitif l'aperitivo (m)
appetite l'appetito (m)
appetizers i primi piatti
apple la mela
application form il modulo per la domanda
appointment l'appuntamento (m)
apricot l'albicocca (f)
April aprile
architecture l'architettura (f)
are: you are (singular, formal) (Lei) è; (singular, informal) (tu) sei; (plural) (voi) siete; *we are* (noi) siamo; *they are* (loro) sono
arm il braccio
armchair la poltrona
arrange (appointment, etc.) fissare
arrivals gli arrivi
arrive arrivare

art l'arte (f)
art gallery la pinacoteca, la galleria d'arte
artist l'artista (m/f)
as: as soon as possible (il) più presto possibile
ashtray il portacenere
asparagus gli asparagi
aspirin l'aspirina (f)
asthmatic asmatico
at: at the post office all'ufficio postale; *at night* di notte; *at 3 o'clock* alle tre
athletic shoes le scarpe da ginnastica
ATM il bancomat
attic la soffitta
attractive attraente
audience gli spettatori
August agosto
aunt la zia
Australia l'Australia (f)
Australian australiano (-a)
automatic automatico
fall l'autunno (m)
away: is it far away? è lontano?; *go away!* vattene!
awful terribile, orribile

B

baby il bambino/la bambina
baby carriage la carrozzina
back (not front) la parte posteriore; (body) la schiena; *to come back* tornare
backpack lo zaino
bacon la pancetta
bad cattivo
bag la borsa, il sacchetto
baggage claim il ritiro bagagli
bait l'esca (f)
bake cuocere (al forno)

bakery la pasticceria
balcony il balcone; (in theater) la galleria
ball (soccer, etc.) la palla, il pallone; (tennis, etc.) la pallina
banana la banana
band (musicians) la banda
bandage la fascia; (adhesive) il cerotto
bank la banca
banknote la banconota
bar (drinks) il bar; *bar of chocolate* la tavoletta di cioccolata
barbecue il barbecue; (occasion) la grigliata all'aperto
barber shop il barbiere
bargain l'affare (m)
basement il seminterrato
basket il cestino; (in supermarket) il cestello
bath: to take a bath fare il bagno
bathroom il bagno
bathtub la vasca
bathroom il bagno
battery la batteria
be (verb) essere
beach la spiaggia
beans i fagioli
beard la barba
beautiful bello
because perché
bed il letto
bed linen le lenzuola
bedroom la camera (da letto)
bedspread il copriletto
beef il manzo
beer la birra
before ... prima di ...
beginner il/la principiante
beginners' slope la discesa per principianti
behind dietro; *behind ...* dietro a ...
beige beige
bell (church) la campana; (door) il campanello
below sotto
belt la cintura
beside ... vicino a ...
best il migliore
better (than) migliore (di)
between ... fra ...
bicycle la bicicletta
big grande
bikini il bikini
bird l'uccello (m)
birthday il compleanno; *happy birthday!* buon compleanno!
bite (by dog) il morso; (by insect) la puntura; (verb: by dog) mordere; (verb: by insect) pungere
bitter amaro
black nero
black currant il ribes nero
blanket la coperta
bleach la varecchina; (verb: hair) ossigenare
blind (cannot see) cieco; (on window) la tenda avvolgibile
blond (adj) biondo/bionda
blood il sangue; *blood test* le analisi del sangue
blouse la camicetta
blue azzurro; (navy blue) blu
boarding pass la carta d'imbarco
boat la nave; (small) la barca; (passenger) il battello
body il corpo
boil (verb: of water) bollire; (egg, etc.) far bollire
boiled lesso
boiler la caldaia
bolt (on door) il catenaccio; (verb) chiudere con il catenaccio
bone l'osso (m); (fish) la lisca
book il libro; (verb) prenotare
booking office la biglietteria
bookstore la libreria
boot lo stivale
border il confine
boring noioso; *that's boring!* che noia!
born nato; *I was born in 1965* sono nato nel 1965; *I was born in London* sono nato a Londra
both of them tutti e due; *both ... and ...* sia ... che ...
bottle la bottiglia
bottle opener l'apribottiglie (m)
bottom il fondo; *at the bottom (of)* in fondo (a)
bowl la scodella, la ciotola; (mixing bowl) la terrina
box la scatola; (of wood, etc.) la cassetta
box office il botteghino
boy il ragazzo
bra il reggiseno
bracelet il braccialetto

brake il freno; (verb) frenare
branch (of company) la filiale
bread il pane
bread shop la panetteria
breakdown (car) il guasto; (nervous) l'esaurimento nervoso (m)
breakfast la colazione
breathe respirare
bridge il ponte
briefcase la cartella
bring portare
British britannico
brochure l'opuscolo (m)
broken rotto; *broken leg* la gamba rotta
brooch la spilla
brother il fratello
brown marrone
bruise il livido
brush (hair) la spazzola; (paint) il pennello; (cleaning) la scopa; (verb: hair) spazzolare
bucket il secchio
budget il budget
building l'edificio (m)
bumper il paraurti
bunker (golf) il bunker
burglar il ladro
burglary il furto
burn la bruciatura; (verb) bruciare
bus l'autobus (m); (long-distance) il pullman
business l'affare (m); *it's none of your business* non sono affari tuoi; *business card* il biglietto da visita
bus station la stazione degli autobus
bus stop la fermata dell'autobus
busy (occupied) occupato; (telephone) occupato; (bar, etc.) animato
but ma
butcher shop la macelleria
butter il burro
button il bottone
buy comprare
by: by the window vicino alla finestra; *by Friday* entro venerdì; *by myself* da solo; *written by ...* scritto da ...

C

cabbage il cavolo
cable car la funivia

café il caffè, il bar
cage la gabbia
cake la torta
calculator il calcolatore
call la chiamata; *what's it called?* come si chiama?
camera la macchina fotografica
camper trailer la roulotte
camper van il camper
campfire il falò
campground il campeggio
camshaft l'albero a camme (m)
can (vessel) la lattina; (verb: to be able) *can I have ...?* posso avere ...?; *can you ...?* potreste ...?
Canada il Canada
Canadian canadese
canal il canale
candle la candela
canoe la canoa
can opener l'apriscatole (m)
cap (bottle) il tappo; (hat) il berretto
car l'auto (m), la macchina
carburetor il carburatore
card (greetings card) il biglietto di auguri; *playing cards* le carte da gioco
careful attento; *be careful!* stia attento!
caretaker il portinaio/la portinaia
carpenter il falegname
carpet il tappeto
carrot la carota
carry out (verb) da portare via
car seat (for a baby) il seggiolino per macchina
cart il carrello
case (suitcase) la valigia
cash il denaro, gli spicci; (verb) riscuotere; *to pay cash* pagare in contanti
cashier il cassiere
cassette la cassetta
cassette player il mangianastri
castle il castello
cat il gatto
cathedral il duomo, la cattedrale
Catholic cattolico
cauliflower il cavolfiore
cave la grotta
CD il compact disc
ceiling il soffitto
cellar la cantina
cell phone il cellulare, il telefonino

cemetery il cimitero
central heating il riscaldamento centrale
center il centro
certificate il certificato
certo certainly
chair la sedia; *swivel chair* la sedia girevole
change (money) il cambio, gli spicci; (verb: money, trains) cambiare; (clothes) cambiarsi
charger il caricabatterie
cheap economico, a buon mercato
check l'assegno (m); (restaurant) il conto
checkbook il libretto degli assegni
check in (verb) fare il check-in
check-in il check-in; *check-in desk* lo sportello del check-in
check-out la cassa
cheers! (toast) alla salute!, cin cin!
cheese il formaggio
cherry la ciliegia
chess gli scacchi
chest (part of body) il petto; (furniture) il baule
chest of drawers il cassettone
chewing gum il chewing-gum
chicken il pollo
child il bambino; (female) la bambina
children i bambini; (own children) i figli; *children's ward* il reparto di pediatria
chimney il comignolo
china la porcellana
chips le patatine
chocolate la cioccolata; *box of chocolates* la scatola di cioccolatini
chop (food) la costoletta; (verb) tagliare (a pezzetti)
Christmas il Natale
church la chiesa
cigar il sigaro
cigarette la sigaretta
city la città
class la classe
classical music la musica classica
clean (adj) pulito; (verb) pulire
cleaner la donna delle pulizie
clear (obvious) chiaro; (water) limpido
clever bravo, intelligente
client il cliente

clock l'orologio (m)
close (near) vicino; (a)(verb) chiudere
closed chiuso
clothes i vestiti
clothespin la molletta
clubs (cards) i fiori
clutch la frizione
coat hanger l'attaccapanni (m)
coat il capotto
coffee il caffè
coin la moneta
cold (illness) il raffreddore; (adj) freddo; *I have a cold* ho un raffreddore
collar il colletto; (for dog) il collare
colleague il collega
collection (stamps, etc.) la collezione
color il colore
color film il rullino a colori
comb il pettine; (verb) pettinare
come venire; *I come from ...* sono di ...; *come here!* (formal/informal) vieni/venga qui!; *come with me* (formal/informal) vieni/venga con me
comforter il piumino
compartment lo scompartimento
complicated complicato
computer il computer; *computer games* i videogiochi
concert il concerto
conditioner (hair) il balsamo
condom il preservativo
conductor (bus) il bigliettaio; (orchestra) il direttore
conference la conferenza; *conference room* la sala conferenze
congratulations! congratulazioni!
connection la coincidenza
consulate il consolato
contact lenses le lenti a contatto
contraceptive il contraccettivo
contract il contratto
cook il cuoco/la cuoca; (verb) cucinare
cookie il biscotto
cool fresco
cork il tappo
corkscrew il cavatappi
corner l'angolo (m)
corridor il corridoio
cosmetics i cosmetici

cost (verb) costare;
what does it cost?
quanto costa?
cotton il cotone
cotton balls il cotone
idrofilo
cough la tosse; (verb)
tossire
countertop il piano di
lavoro
country (state) il paese;
(not town) la
campagna
course (educational)
il corso
cousin il cugino/la
cugina
crab il granchio
cramp il crampo
crayfish il gambero
crazy pazzo
cream (dairy) la crema,
la panna; (lotion) la
crema
credit card la carta di
credito
crew l'equipaggio (m)
crib il lettino
croissant la brioche
crowded affollato
cruise la crociera
crutches le stampelle
cry (to weep) piangere;
(to shout) gridare
cucumber il cetriolo
cufflinks i gemelli
cup la tazza
cupboard l'armadio (m)
curlers i bigodini
curls i ricci
curtain la tenda
cushion il cuscino
customs la dogana
cut il taglio; (verb)
tagliare

D

dad il papà, il babbo
dairy la latteria; *dairy
products* i latticini
damp umido
dance il ballo; (verb)
ballare
dangerous pericoloso
dark scuro
daughter la figlia
day il giorno
dead morto
deaf sordo
dear caro
debit card la carta
assegni
December dicembre
deck (of cards) il mazzo
di carte
decorator l'imbianchino
deep profondo
*degree: I have a degree
in* ... sono laureato in ...
delayed in ritardo

deliberately
deliberatamente
delicatessen la salumeria
delivery la consegna
dentist il/la dentista
dentures la dentiera
deodorant il deodorante
department il reparto
department store il
grande magazzino
departure la partenza;
departures le
partenze; *departure
lounge* la sala d'attesa
designer il grafico/la
grafica
desk la scrivania
desserts i dessert
develop (film) sviluppare
diabetic diabetico
diamond (jewel) il
diamante
diamonds (cards)
i quadri
diapers i pannolini
diarrhea la diarrea
dictionary il dizionario
die morire
diesel il gasolio
different diverso; *that's
different!* è diverso!;
I'd like a different one
ne vorrei un altro
difficult difficile
dining room la sala da
pranzo
dinner la cena
directory (telephone)
la guida telefonica
dirty sporco
disabled (people)
i disabili
discount la riduzione
discount rate la tariffa
ridotta
dishtowel lo strofinaccio
dishwasher la
lavastoviglie
dishwashing liquid il
detersivo per i piatti
dive il tuffo; (verb)
tuffarsi
diving board il
trampolino
divorced divorziato
do fare; *how do you do?*
piacere di conoscerla;
what do you do? che
lavoro fa?
dock il molo
doctor (academic) il
dottore/la dottoressa;
(medical) il medico
document il documento
dog il cane; *dog basket*
la cuccia; *dog bowl* la
ciotola del cane
doll la bambola
dollar il dollaro
door la porta; (of car)
lo sportello

double room la
matrimoniale, la
camera doppia
doughnut il krapfen
down giù
downtown il centro città
drawer il cassetto
dress il vestito
drink la bibita; (verb)
bere; *would you like
a drink?* vorresti
qualcosa da bere?
drinking water l'acqua
potabile (f)
drive (verb) guidare
driver il guidatore/la
guidatrice; (of bus,
truck, etc.) l'autista
(m/f)
driver's license la
patente (di guida)
driveway il viale
drops le gocce
drunk ubriaco
dry asciutto; (wine)
secco
dry-cleaner's la
lavanderia a secco
during durante
duster lo straccio per la
polvere

E

each (every) ogni;
twenty euros each
venti euro ciascuno
ear l'orecchio (m); *ears*
le orecchie
early presto; *see you
soon* a presto
earphones gli auricolari
earrings gli orecchini
east l'est (m)
easy facile
eat mangiare
egg l'uovo (m)
eight otto
eighteen diciotto
eighty ottanta
either: either of them
l'uno o l'altro
elastic elastico
elbow il gomito
electric elettrico;
electrical hookup la
presa di corrente
electrician il/la
elettricista
electricity l'elettricità (f)
elevator l'ascensore (m)
eleven undici
else: something else
qualcos'altro; *someone
else* qualcun'altro;
somewhere else da
qualche altra parte
email l'email (f), la
posta elettronica
email address l'indirizzo
di posta elettronica (m)

embarrassing imbarazzante

embassy l'ambasciata (f)

emergency l'emergenza (f)

emergency exit l'uscita di sicurezza (f)

emergency department il pronto soccorso

empty vuoto

end la fine

engaged (to be married) fidanzato/ fidanzata

engine (car) il motore; (train) la locomotiva

engineering l'ingegneria

England l'Inghilterra (f)

English inglese

enlargement l'ampliamento (m)

enough abbastanza

entrance l'entrata (f)

envelope la busta

epileptic epilettico

eraser la gomma

escalator la scala mobile

especially particolarmente

estimate il preventivo

evening la sera

every ogni; *every day* tutti i giorni

everyone ognuno, tutti

everything tutto

everywhere dappertutto

example l'esempio (m); *for example* per esempio

excellent ottimo, eccellente

excess baggage il bagaglio in eccesso

exchange (verb) scambiare

exchange rate il (tasso di) cambio

excursion l'escursione (f)

excuse me! (to get past) permesso!; (to get attention) mi scusi!; (when sneezing, etc.) scusate!

executive il dirigente

exhaust (car) la marmitta

exhibition la mostra

exit l'uscita (f)

expensive caro, costoso

expressway l'autostrada (f)

extension cord la prolunga

eye l'occhio (m); *eyes* gli occhi

eyebrow il sopracciglio

F

face la faccia

faint (unclear) indistinto; (verb) svenire

fair (funfair) il luna park; (trade) la fiera (commerciale); *it's not fair* non è giusto

false teeth la dentiera

family la famiglia

fan (ventilator) il ventilatore; (enthusiast) l'ammiratore (m)

fan belt la cinghia della ventola

fantastic fantastico

far lontano; *how far is it to ...?* quanto dista da qui ...?

fare il biglietto, la tariffa

farm la fattoria

farmer l'agricoltore (m)

fashion la moda

fast veloce

fat il grasso; (adj) grasso

father il padre

fax il fax; (verb) spedire via fax

fax machine il fax

February febbraio

feel (touch) tastare; *I feel hot* ho caldo; *I feel like ...* ho voglia di ...; *I don't feel well* non mi sento bene

fence lo steccato

fennel il finocchio

ferry il traghetto

fever la febbre

fiancé il fidanzato

fiancée la fidanzata

field il campo

fifteen quindici

fifty cinquanta

figures le cifre

filling (in tooth) l'otturazione (f); (in sandwich, cake, etc.) il ripieno

film (for camera) la pellicola; (at the movies) il film

filter il filtro

financial consultant il/la consulente finanziario

fine! benissimo!

finger il dito

fire il fuoco; (blaze) l'incendio (m)

fire extinguisher l'estintore (m)

fireplace il caminetto

fireworks i fuochi d'artificio

first primo; *first class* prima classe

first aid il pronto soccorso

first name il nome di battesimo

fish il pesce

fishing la pesca; *to go fishing* andare a pesca

fishmonger (shop) la pescheria

five cinque

fizzy frizzante

flag la bandiera

flash (camera) il flash

flat (level) piatto; (apartment) l'appartamento

flavor il gusto

flashlight la torcia (elettrica)

flea la pulce

flight il volo; *flight number* il numero del volo

flipflops gli infradito

flippers le pinne

floor (ground) il pavimento; (story) il piano

Florence Firenze

flour la farina

flower il fiore; *flower bed* l'aiuola (f)

flute il flauto

fly (insect) la mosca; (verb) volare; *I'm flying to London* vado a Londra in aereo

flysheet il telo protettivo

fog la nebbia

folk music la musica folk

food il cibo

food poisoning l'intossicazione alimentare (f)

foot il piede; *on foot* a piedi

for per; *for me* per me; *what for?* perché?

forbidden proibito

foreigner lo straniero, il forestiero

forest la foresta

forget dimenticare

fork (for food) la forchetta

forty quaranta

four quattro

fourteen quattordici

fourth quarto

fracture la frattura

France la Francia

free (not occupied) libero; (no charge) gratuito, gratis

freezer il congelatore

French francese

french fries le patatine fritte

Friday venerdì

fried fritto

friend l'amico; (female) l'amica

friendly cordiale

frightened: I'm frightened ho paura

front: in front of you davanti a te

frost il gelo

frozen foods i surgelati
fruit la frutta
fruit juice il succo di frutta
fry friggere
frying pan la padella
full pieno; *I'm full* sono sazio
full board la pensione completa
funny divertente; (odd) strano
furniture i mobili

G

garage il garage
garbage le immondizie, la spazzatura
garbage bag il sacchetto per la pattumiera
garbage can la pattumiera
garden il giardino; *garden center* il vivaio
gardener il giardiniere
garlic l'aglio (m)
gasoline la benzina
gas-permeable lenses le lenti semi-rigide
gas station il benzinaio, la stazione di servizio
gate il cancello; (at airport) l'uscita (f)
gay (homosexual) omosessuale, gay
gearbox (car) il cambio
gear stick la leva del cambio
gel (hair) il gel
Genoa Genova
German tedesco
Germany la Germania
get (obtain) ricevere; (fetch: person) chiamare; (something) prendere; *do you have ...?* ha ...?; *to get the train* prendere il treno
get back: we get back tomorrow torniamo domani; *to get something back* riavere indietro qualcosa
get in entrare; (arrive) arrivare
get off (bus, etc.) scendere (da)
get on (bus, etc.) salire (su)
get out uscire (da)
get up alzarsi
gift il regalo
gin il gin
ginger (spice) lo zenzero
girl la ragazza
give dare
glad contento

glass (material) il vetro; (for drinking) il bicchiere
glasses gli occhiali
gloves i guanti
glue la colla
go andare; (depart) partire
gold l'oro (m)
golf il golf
golfer il golfista
good buono; *good! bene!*
goodbye arrivederci
good day buongiorno
good evening buonasera
good night buonanotte
government il governo
granddaughter la nipote
grandfather il nonno
grandmother la nonna
grandparents i nonni
grandson il nipote
grapes l'uva (f)
grass l'erba (f)
gray grigio
great! benissimo!
Great Britain la Gran Bretagna
Greece la Grecia
Greek greco
green verde
grill la griglia
grilled alla griglia
grocery store gli alimentari
ground floor il pianterreno
groundsheet il telone impermeabile
guarantee la garanzia; (verb) garantire
guard la guardia
guest l'ospite (m/f)
guide (person) la guida
guidebook la guida
guitar la chitarra
gun (rifle) il fucile; (pistol) la pistola
gutter la grondaia
guy rope la corda
gymnastics la palestra

H

hair i capelli
haircut il taglio
hairdresser il parrucchiere
hair dryer il fohn
hairspray la lacca per i capelli
half metà; *half an hour* mezz'ora; *half board* mezza pensione; *half past ... ...* e mezza
ham il prosciutto
hamburger l'hamburger (m)
hammer il martello
hamster il criceto

hand brake il freno a mano
hand la mano; *hand luggage* il bagaglio a mano
handle (door) la maniglia
handshake la stretta di mano
handsome bello, attraente
handyman il muratore
hangover i postumi della sbornia
happy felice, contento
harbor il porto
hard duro; (difficult) difficile
hardware store la ferramenta
hat il cappello
have avere; *I don't have ...* non ho ...; *do you have ...?* ha ...?; *I have to go now* devo andare adesso
he lui
head la testa
headache il mal di testa
headlights i fari
headquarters la sede centrale
hear udire, sentire
hearing aid l'apparecchio acustico (m)
heart il cuore
heart condition il disturbi cardiaci
hearts (cards) i cuori
heater il termosifone
heating il riscaldamento
heavy pesante
hedge la siepe
heel (of foot) il tallone; (of shoe) il tacco
hello ciao, buongiorno; (on phone) pronto
help l'aiuto (m); (verb) aiutare; *can I help you?* dica?
her lei, suo, sua, suoi; *it's for her* è per lei; *her book* il suo libro; *her house* la sua casa; *her shoes* le sue scarpe; *her dresses* i suoi vestiti; *it's hers* è suo
herbal tea la tisana
here qui
here you are/here it is ecco
hi! Ciao!
high alto
hiking l'escursionismo
hill la collina
him: it's for him è per lui; *give it to him* daglielo
his suo, sua, sue, suoi; *his book* il suo libro; *his house* la sua casa;

his shoes le sue scarpe; *his socks* i suoi calzini; *it's his* è suo
history la storia
hitchhike fare l'autostop
HIV-positive HIV positivo
hobby il passatempo, il hobby
holiday il giorno festivo
home: *at home* a casa
homeopathy omeopatia
honest onesto
honey il miele
honeymoon la luna di miele
hood (car) il cofano
horn (car) il clacson; (animal) il corno
horrible orribile
hose il tubo
hospital l'ospedale (m)
host il padrone di casa; *hostess* la padrona di casa
hot caldo
hour l'ora (f); *visiting hours* l'orario di visita (f)
house la casa
household products gli articoli per la casa
how? come?
how much? quanto costa?; *how much is that?* quant'è?
hundred cento; *three hundred* trecento
hungry: *I'm hungry* ho fame
hurry affrettarsi; *I'm in a hurry* ho fretta
hurry up! sbrigati!
hurt: *my ... hurts* mi fa male il/la ...; *will it hurt?* farà male?
husband il marito

I

I io
ice il ghiaccio
ice cream il gelato
ice skates i pattini da ghiaccio
identification il documento d'identità
if se
ignition l'accensione (f)
ill malato
immediately immediatamente
impossible impossibile
in: *in English* in inglese; *in the hotel* nell'albergo; *in Venice* a Venezia
included incluso
indigestion l'indigestione (f)
infection l'infezione (f)
information le informazioni; *information technology* l'informatica (f)
inhaler (for asthma, etc.) l'inalatore (m)
injection l'iniezione (m)
injury la ferita
ink l'inchiostro (m)
in-laws i suoceri
inner tube la camera d'aria
insect l'insetto (m)
insect repellent l'insettifugo (m)
insomnia l'insonnia (f)
instant coffee il caffè solubile
insurance l'assicurazione (f)
interesting interessante
Internet l'internet (f)
interpret interpretare
interpreter l'interprete (m/f)
intersection l'incrocio (m)
intravenous drip la flebo
invitation l'invito (m)
invoice la fattura
Ireland l'Irlanda (f)
Irish irlandese
iron (material) il ferro; (for clothes) il ferro da stiro; (verb) stirare
is: *he/she/it is ...* (lui/lei/esso) è ...
island l'isola (f)
it esso
Italian italiano
Italy Italia
its suo

J

jacket la giacca
jam la marmellata
January gennaio
jazz il jazz
jeans i jeans
jellyfish la medusa
jeweler (shop) il gioielliere
job il lavoro
jog (verb) fare jogging; *to go jogging* andare a fare jogging
jogging il jogging
jogging suit la tuta da ginnastica
joke lo scherzo
journey il viaggio
July luglio
June giugno
just (only) solo; *it's just arrived* è appena arrivato

K

kerosene la paraffina
key la chiave

keyboard la tastiera
kidney il rene
kilo il chilo
kilometer il chilometro
kitchen la cucina
knee il ginocchio
knife il coltello
knit lavorare a maglia
knitwear la maglieria
know conoscere; (person) conoscere; *I don't know* non so

L

label l'etichetta (f)
lace il pizzo
laces (of shoe) i lacci
lady la signora
lake il lago
lamb l'agnello (m)
lamp la lampada
lampshade il paralume
land la terra; (verb) atterrare
language la lingua
laptop (computer) il computer portatile
large grande
last (final) ultimo; *last week* la settimana scorsa; *at last!* finalmente!
last name il cognome
late: *it's getting late* si sta facendo tardi; *the bus is late* l'autobus è in ritardo
later più tardi
laugh ridere
laundry (place) la lavanderia; (dirty clothes) la biancheria
laundry detergent il detersivo (per bucato)
law la legge
lawn il prato; *lawnmower* il tosaerba
lawyer l'avvocato
laxative il lassativo
lazy pigro
leaf la foglia
leaflet il volantino
learn imparare
leash (for dog) il guinzaglio
leather la pelle, il cuoio; *leather goods shop* la pelletteria
lecture hall l'aula delle lezioni (f)
left (not right) sinistra; *there's nothing left* non c'è rimasto più nulla
left luggage locker il deposito bagagli
leg la gamba
lemon il limone
lemonade la limonata

length la lunghezza

lens la lente

less meno

lesson la lezione

letter la lettera

lettuce la lattuga

library la biblioteca

license la patente

license plate la targa

life la vita

light la luce; (not heavy) leggero; (not dark) chiaro

light bulb la lampadina

lighter l'accendino (m)

lighter fuel il gas per accendini

light meter l'esposimetro (m)

like: I like ... mi piace ...; *it's like ...* assomiglia a ...; *like this one* come questo

lime (fruit) il limoncello

line (telephone, etc.) la linea; *outside line* linea esterna

line (waiting) la fila; *stand in line* fare la fila

lipstick il rossetto

liqueur il liquore

list l'elenco (m)

liter il litro

literature la letteratura

litter (bin) i rifiuti

little (small) piccolo; *it's a little big* è un po' grande; *just a little* solo un po'

liver il fegato

living room il soggiorno

lollipop il lecca lecca

long lungo; *how long does it take?* quanto ci vuole?

long-distance (call) interurbana

lost: I'm lost mi sono persa

lost property l'ufficio oggetti smarriti (m)

lot: a lot molto

loud forte

love (verb) amare

low basso

luck la fortuna; *good luck!* buona fortuna!

luggage i bagagli

luggage rack la reticella (per i bagagli)

lunch il pranzo

M

madam signora

magazine la rivista

maid la cameriera

mail la posta; (verb) spedire per posta

mailbox la cassetta delle lettere

mail carrier il postino

main courses i secondi piatti

make fare

makeup il trucco

man l'uomo; *men* gli uomini

manager il direttore/la direttrice

many molti; *not many* non molti

map la carta (geografica); (of town) la pianta

marble il marmo

March marzo

margarine la margarina

market il mercato

marmalade la marmellata d'arance

married sposato

mascara il mascara

mass (church) la messa

mast l'albero (m)

match (light) il fiammifero; (sports) l'incontro (m)

material (cloth) la stoffa

matter: it doesn't matter non importa; *what's the matter* cosa c'è?

mattress il materasso

May maggio

maybe forse

me: it's me sono io; *it's for me* è per me

meal il pasto

mean: what does this mean? che cosa significa?

meat la carne

mechanic il meccanico

medicine la medicina

Mediterranean il Mediterraneo

meeting la riunione, l'incontro (m)

melon il melone

menu il menù

message il messaggio

microwave il forno a microonde

middle: in the middle of the square in mezzo alla piazza; *in the middle of the night* nel cuore della notte

midnight mezzanotte

Milan Milano

milk il latte

million milione

mine: it's mine è mio

mineral water l'acqua minerale (f)

minute il minuto

mirror lo specchio

Miss Signorina

mistake l'errore (m)

modem il modem

mom mamma

Monday lunedì

money i soldi

monitor (computer) il monitor

month il mese

monument il monumento

moon la luna

moped il motorino

more più; *more than ...* più di ...

morning la mattina; *in the morning* di mattina

mosaic il mosaico

mosquito la zanzara

mother la madre

motorboat il motoscafo

motorcycle la motocicletta

mountain la montagna

mountain bike mountain bike

mouse (animal) il topo; (computer) il mouse

mousse (for hair) la schiuma

mouth la bocca

move muovere; *don't move!* non muoverti!

move house traslocare

movie theater il cinema

Mr. Signor

Mrs. Signora

much molto; *much better* molto meglio; *much slower* molto più lentamente; *not much* non molto

mug il tazzone

museum il museo

mushroom il fungo

music la musica

musical instrument lo strumento musicale

musician il musicista

music system lo stereo

mussels le cozze

must (to have to) devore; *I must* devo

mustache i baffi

mustard la senape

my mio, mia, mie, miei; *my book* il mio libro; *my bag* la mia borsa; *my keys* le mie chiavi; *my dresses* i miei vestiti

N

nail (metal) il chiodo; (finger) l'unghia (f)

nail clippers il tagliaunghie

nail file la limetta per le unghie

nail polish lo smalto per le unghie

name il nome; *what's your name?* come si chiama/ti chiami? (formal/informal);

my name's ... mi chiamo...
napkin il tovagliolo
Naples Napoli
narrow stretto
near vicino; *near to* ... vicino a ...
necessary necessario, obbligatorio
neck il collo
necklace la collana
need avere bisogno; *I need* ... ho bisogno di ...; *there's no need* non c'è bisogno
needle l'ago (m)
negative (photo) la negativa; (adj) negativo
nephew il nipote
never mai
new nuovo
news le notizie; (on radio) il notiziario
newsstand il giornalaio
newspaper il giornale
New Zealand la Nuova Zelanda
New Zealander neozelandese
next prossimo; *next week* la settimana prossima; *what next?* e poi?; *who's next?* a chi tocca?
nice (attractive) carino, bello; (pleasant) simpatico; (to eat) buono
niece la nipote
night la notte
nightclub il night
nightgown la camicia da notte
nightstand il comodino
nine nove
nineteen diciannove
ninety novanta
no (negative response) no; *I have no money* non ho soldi
nobody nessuno
no entry divieto di accesso
noisy rumoroso
noon il mezzogiorno
north il nord
Northern Ireland l'Irlanda del Nord
nose il naso
not non; *he's not* ... non è ...
notebook il quaderno
notepad il bloc-notes
nothing niente
novel il romanzo
November novembre
now ora, adesso
nowhere da nessuna parte

number il numero
nurse l'infermiere/la infermiera
nut la noce, la nocciola; (for bolt) il dado

O

oars i remi
occasionally ogni tanto
occupied occupato
o'clock: one o'clock l'una; *two o'clock* le due
occupied (restroom) occupato
October ottobre
octopus la piovra, il polipo
of di
office l'ufficio (m), la direzione; *office worker* l'impiegato/a
often spesso
oil l'olio (m)
ointment la pomata, l'unguento (m)
OK OK
old vecchio; *how old are you?* quanti anni hai?
olive l'oliva (f)
olive oil l'olio d'oliva (m)
omelet l'omelette (f)
on su; *a book on Venice* un libro su Venezia; *on Monday* di lunedì
one uno
one way senso unico
one-way ticket il biglietto di sola andata
onion la cipolla
only solo
open (adj) aperto; (verb) aprire
opera l'opera (f)
operating room la sala operatoria
operation l'operazione (f)
operator l'operatore/l'operatrice (m/f)
opposite davanti a
optician l'ottico (m)
or o
orange (fruit) l'arancia (f); (color) arancione
orange juice il succo d'arancia
orchestra l'orchestra (f); (theater seating) la platea
order (for goods) l'ordinativo (m), l'ordine (m)
ordinary normale
organ (music) l'organo (m)
other: the other (one) l'altro

our: our hotel il nostro albergo; *our car* la nostra macchina; *it's ours* è nostro
out: he's out è uscito
outside fuori
oven il forno
over (above) su, sopra; *over 100* più di cento; *over the river* al di là del fiume; *it's over* (finished) è finito; *over there* laggiù
overpass il cavalcavia

P

pacifier (for baby) il ciuccio
package, packet il pacchetto
padlock il lucchetto
Padua Padova
page la pagina
pain il dolore
paint la vernice
painting la pittura
pair il paio
pajamas il pigiama
palace il palazzo
pale pallido
paper la carta; (newspaper) il giornale
pants i pantaloni
pantyhose (sheer) i collant
parcel il pacco
pardon? prego?
parents i genitori
park il parco; (verb) parcheggiare; *no parking* sosta vietata
parking lights le luci di posizione
parking lot il parcheggio
parsley il prezzemolo
part (hair) la riga
party (celebration) la festa; (group) il gruppo; (political) il partito
pass (driving) sorpassare
passenger il passeggero; (female) la passeggera
passport il passaporto; *passport control* il controllo passaporti
password la password
pasta la pasta
path il vialetto, il sentiero
pay pagare
payment il pagamento
peach la pesca
peanuts le arachidi
pear la pera
pearl la perla
peas i piselli

pedestrian il pedone

pedestrian zone la zona pedonale

peg (tent) il picchetto

pen la penna

pencil la matita

pencil sharpener il temperamatite

penicillin la penicillina

penknife il temperino

pen pal il/la corrispondente

people la gente

pepper (spice)il pepe; (vegetable) il peperone

peppermint la menta piperita

per: per person a persona; *per annum* all'anno

perfect perfetto

perfume il profumo

perhaps magari, forse

perm la permanente

pharmacy la farmacia

phone card la scheda telefonica

photocopier la fotocopiatrice

photograph la fotografia; (verb) fotografare

photographer il fotografo

phrasebook il vocabolarietto

pickpocket il borsaiolo

pickup (postal) la levata

picnic il picnic

piece il pezzo

pillow il guanciale

PIN il pin, il codice segreto

pin lo spillo

pineapple l'ananas (m)

pink rosa

pipe (for smoking) la pipa; (for water) il tubo

piston il pistone

place il posto; *at your place* a casa tua

planner l'agenda (f)

plans le piante

plant la pianta

plastic la plastica

plastic bag il sacchetto di plastica

plate il piatto

platform il binario

play (theater) la commedia; (verb) giocare

please per favore

pleased to meet you piacere

plug (electrical) la spina; (sink) il tappo

plumber il idraulico

pocket la tasca

poison il veleno

police la polizia

police officer il poliziotto

police report il rapporto di polizia

police station la stazione di polizia

politics la politica

poor povero

poor quality di cattiva qualità

pop music la musica pop

Pope il Papa

pork la carne di maiale

port il porto

porter (hotel) il portiere

possible possibile

postcard la cartolina

post office l'ufficio postale (m)

potato la patata

poultry il pollame

pound (weight) la libbra; (currency) la sterlina

prefer preferire

pregnant incinta

prescription la ricetta

presentation la conferenza

pretty (beautiful) grazioso, carino; (quite) piuttosto

price il prezzo

priest il prete

printer la stampante

private privato

problem il problema; *no problem* non c'è problema

profits i profitti

public pubblico

pull tirare

puncture la foratura

purple viola

purse il borsellino

push spingere

pushchair il passegino

put mettere

Q

quality la qualità

quarter il quarto; *quarter past ...* ... e un quarto

question la domanda

quick veloce

quiet tranquillo

quite (fairly) abbastanza; (fully) molto

R

rabbit il coniglio (m)

radiator il radiatore

radio la radio

radish il ravanello

railroad la ferrovia

rain la pioggia

raincoat l'impermeabile (m)

raisins l'uvetta (f)

rake il rastrello

rare (uncommon) raro; (meat) al sangue

rash il arrossamento

raspberry il lampone

rat il ratto

razor blades le lamette

read leggere

reading lamp la lampada da studio

ready pronto

realtor l'agente immobiliare (m/f)

rear lights i fari posteriori

receipt (restaurants, hotels) la ricevuta; (shops, bars) lo scontrino

reception (party) il rinfresco; (hotel) la reception

receptionist il/la receptionist

record (music) il disco; (sports, etc.) il record

record store il negozio di dischi

red rosso

refreshments i rinfreschi

refrigerator il frigorifero

registered (mail) raccomandata

relax rilassarsi

relief: what a relief! che sollievo!

religion la religione

remember ricordare; *I don't remember* non ricordo

rent (verb) affittare, noleggiare

repair riparare

report la relazione

research la ricerca

reservation la prenotazione

rest (noun: remainder) il resto; (verb: to relax) riposarsi

restaurant il ristorante

return ritornare; (give back) restituire

rice il riso

rich ricco

right (correct) giusto, esatto; (not left) destro

ring (jewelry) l'anello (m)

ripe maturo

river il fiume

road la strada

roasted arrosto

rock (stone) la roccia; (music) il rock

roll (bread) il panino

Rome Roma

roof il tetto

room la stanza, la camera; (space) lo spazio; *room service* il servizio in camera
rope la corda
rose la rosa
round (circular) rotondo
roundabout la rotatoria
round-trip ticket il biglietto di andata e ritorno
row remare
rubber band l'elastico (m)
ruby (gem) il rubino
rug (mat) il tappeto
rugby il rugby
ruins le rovine, i resti
ruler (for drawing) la riga
rum il rum
run (verb) correre

S

sad triste
safe (not dangerous) sicuro
safety pin la spilla di sicurezza
sailing la vela
salad l'insalata (f)
salami il salame
sale (at reduced prices) i saldi
sales (of goods, etc.) le vendite
salmon il salmone
salt il sale
same: the same dress lo stesso vestito; *same again, please* un altro, per favore
sand la sabbia
sandals i sandali
sand dunes le dune
sandwich il panino
sanitary napkins gli assorbenti (igienici)
Sardinia la Sardegna
Saturday sabato
sauce la salsa
saucepan la pentola
saucer il piattino
sauna la sauna
sausage la salsiccia
say dire; *what did you say?* che cosa ha detto?; *how do you say ...?* come si dice ...?
scarf la sciarpa; (head) il foulard
schedule l'orario (m)
school la scuola
science la scienza
scissors le forbici
Scotland la Scozia
Scotsman lo scozzese
Scotswoman la scozzese
Scottish scozzese

screen lo schermo
screw la vite
screwdriver il cacciavite
sea il mare
seafood i frutti di mare
seat il posto
seat belt la cintura di sicurezza
second secondo; *second class* seconda classe; *second floor* il primo piano
secretary il segretario/la segretaria
see vedere; *I can't see* non vedo; *I see* (understand) capisco, vedo
self-employed libero professionista
sell vendere
seminar il seminario
send mandare
separate (adj) separato
separated (couple) separati
September settembre
serious serio; (illness) grave
seven sette
seventeen diciassette
seventy settanta
several diversi
sew cucire
shampoo lo shampoo
shave (verb) radersi
shaving cream la schiuma da barba
shawl lo scialle
she lei
sheers le cesoie
sheet il lenzuolo
shell la conchiglia
shellfish (crabs, etc.) i crostacei; (mollusks) i molluschi
sherry lo sherry
ship la nave
shirt la camicia
shoelaces i lacci per le scarpe
shoe polish il lucido per le scarpe
shoe repairer il calzolaio
shoes le scarpe
shop il negozio
shopkeeper il/la commerciante
shopping lo shopping, la spesa; *to go shopping* andare a fare acquisti; (for food) andare a fare la spesa
short basso, corto
shorts gli short
shoulder la spalla
shower la doccia; (rain) l'acquazzone (m)
shower gel la docciaschiuma (f)
shutter (camera)

l'otturatore (m); (window) l'imposta (f), le persiane
Sicily la Sicilia
side (edge) il lato
sidewalk il marciapiede
sign (in station, etc.) il cartello; (road, etc.) l'insegna (f)
sign (verb) firmare
silk la seta
silver (color) d'argento; (metal) l'argento (m)
simple semplice
sing cantare
single (one) solo; (unmarried: man) celibe; (woman) nubile
single room la camera singola
sink il lavabo, il lavandino; (kitchen) il lavello
sir signore
sister la sorella
site (in campground, etc.) la piazzola
six sei
sixteen sedici
sixty sessanta
size (clothes) la taglia; (shoe) il numero
skid slittare
skiing: to go skiing andare a sciare
skin cleanser il latte detergente
ski resort la località sciistica
skirt la gonna
skis gli sci
sky il cielo
sleep il sonno; (verb) dormire
sleeper car il vagone letto
sleeping bag il sacco a pelo
sleeping pill il sonnifero
sleeve la manica
slippers le pantofole
slow lento
small piccolo
smell l'odore (m); (verb: to stink) puzzare
smile il sorriso; (verb) sorridere
smoke il fumo; (verb) fumare
smoking (section) fumatori; *nonsmoking* non fumatori
snack lo spuntino
snorkel il boccaglio
snow la neve
so così; *so good* così bene; *not so much* non così tanto

soaking solution (for contact lenses) il liquido per lenti

soap il sapone

soccer (game) il calcio; (ball) il pallone

socks i calzini

soda water l'acqua di seltz (f)

sofa il divano

soft morbido

soil la terra

somebody qualcuno

somehow in qualche modo

something qualcosa

sometimes qualche volta

somewhere da qualche parte

son il figlio

song la canzone

sorry! scusi!; I'm sorry mi dispiace, spiacente; *sorry?* (pardon) come?, scusi?

soup la minestra, la zuppa

south il sud

souvenir il souvenir

spade (shovel) la vanga

spades (cards) le picche

Spain la Spagna

Spanish spagnolo

spare parts (car) i pezzi di ricambio

spark plug la candela

sparkling water l'acqua gassata (f)

speak parlare; *do you speak ...?* parla ...?; *I don't speak ...* non parlo ...

speed la velocità

SPF (sun protection factor) il fattore di protezione

spider il ragno

spinach gli spinaci

spoon il cucchiaio

sports lo sport

spring (mechanical) la molla; (season) la primavera

square (noun: in town) la piazza; (adj: shape) quadrato

staircase la scala

stairs le scale

stamp il francobollo

stapler la cucitrice, la spillatrice

star la stella; (film) la star

start l'inizio (m); (verb) cominciare

statement (to police) la denuncia

station la stazione

statue la statua

steal rubare; *it's been stolen* è stato rubato

steamed a vapore

steamer (boat) la nave a vapore; (for cooking) la pentola a pressione

still water l'acqua naturale (f)

stockings le calze

stomach lo stomaco

stomachache il mal di pancia

stop (noun: bus) la fermata dell'autobus; (verb) fermare; *stop!* alt!, fermo!

storm la tempesta

stove il cucina

stove fuel il gas da campeggio

straight ahead sempre dritto

strawberry la fragola

stream il ruscello

street la strada

string (cord) lo spago; (guitar, etc.) la corda

strong forte

student lo studente/la studentessa (m/f)

stuffy soffocante

stupid stupido

suburbs la periferia

subway la metro(politana)

sugar lo zucchero

suit il completo; *it suits you* ti sta bene

suitcase la valigia

summer l'estate (f)

sun il sole

sunbathe prendere il sole

sunburn l'eritema solare (m)

Sunday domenica

sunglasses gli occhiali da sole

sunny: it's sunny c'è il sole

sunshade l'ombrellone (m)

suntan: to get a suntan abbronzarsi

suntan lotion la lozione solare

suntanned abbronzato

supermarket il supermercato

supper la cena

supplement il supplemento

suppository la supposta

sure sicuro; *are you sure?* sei sicuro?

sweat il sudore; (verb) sudare

sweater il maglione

sweatshirt la felpa

sweet la caramella; (not sour) dolce

swim (verb) nuotare

swimming il nuoto

swimming pool la piscina

swimming trunks il costume da bagno (per uomo)

swimsuit il costume da bagno

Swiss lo svizzerola/la svizzera; (adj) svizzero

switch l'interruttore (m)

Switzerland la Svizzera

synagogue la sinagoga

syrup lo sciroppo

T

table il tavolo

tablet la compressa

take prendere

takeoff il decollo

talcum powder il talco

talk la conversazione; (verb) parlare

tall alto

tampons i tamponi

tangerine il mandarino

tap il rubinetto

tapestry l'arazzo (m)

taxi il taxi

taxi stand il posteggio dei taxi

tea il tè; *tea with milk* il tè con latte

teach insegnare

teacher l'insegnante

teakettle il bollitore

technician il tecnico

telephone il telefono; (verb) telefonare

telephone booth la cabina telefonica

telephone call la telefonata

telephone number il numero di telefono

television la televisione

temperature la temperatura; (fever) la febbre

ten dieci

tennis il tennis

tent la tenda

tent pole il palo della tenda

terminal (airport) il terminale

terrace il patio

test il controllo

than di

thank (verb) ringraziare; *thank you/thanks* grazie

that: that one quello; *that country* quel paese; *that man* quell'uomo; *that woman* quella donna; *what's that?* cos'è quello?; *I think that ...* penso che ...; *that'll be all* basta così

the il/lo (m); la (f); i/gli (m pl); le (f pl)

theater il teatro

their: their room la loro stanza; *their friend* il loro amico; *their books* i loro libri; *their pens* le loro penne; *it's theirs* è loro

them: it's for them è per loro; *give it to them* dallo a loro

then poi, allora

there là; *there is/are ...* c'è/ci sono ...; *is/are there ...?* c'è/ci sono ...?

these: these things queste cose; *these boys* questi ragazzi

they loro

thick spesso

thief il ladro

thin magro

think pensare; *I think so* penso di sì; *I'll think about it* ci penserò

third terzo

thirsty: I'm thirsty ho sete

thirteen tredici

thirty trenta

this: this one questo; *this picture* questo quadro; *this man* quest'uomo; *this woman* questa donna; *what's this?* cos'è questo?; *this is Mr ...* (questo è) il signor ...

those: those things quelle cose; *those boys* quei ragazzi

thousand mille

three tre

throat la gola

throat lozenges le pasticche per la gola

through attraverso

thumbtack la puntina da disegno

thunderstorm il temporale

Thursday giovedì

Tiber il Tevere

ticket il biglietto

ticket office la biglietteria

tide la marea

tie la cravatta; (verb) legare

tight (clothes) stretto

tights (wool) la calzamaglia

tile la piastrella

time il tempo; *what's time is it?* che ore sono?; *opening times* l'orario di apertura (m) ; *leisure time* il tempo libero

tin la scatola

tip (money) la mancia; (end) la punta

tire la gomma; *flat tire* la gomma a terra*tired* stanco

tissues i fazzolettini di carta

to: to England in Inghilterra; *to the station* alla stazione; *to the doctor* dal dottore; *to the center* in centro

toast il pane tostato

tobacco il tabacco

tobacconist (shop) il tabaccaio

today oggi

together insieme

toilet la toilette

toilet paper la carta igienica

tomato il pomodoro

tomato juice il succo di pomodoro

tomorrow domani; *see you tomorrow* a domani

tongue la lingua

tonic l'acqua tonica (f)

tonight stasera

too (also) anche; (excessively) troppo

tooth il dente

toothache il mal di denti

toothbrush lo spazzolino da denti

toothpaste il dentifricio

tour il giro; *guided tour* la visita guidata

tourist il/la turista

tourist information l'azienda turistica (f); (office) l'ufficio turistico (m)

towel l'asciugamano (m)

tower la torre; *Leaning Tower of Pisa* la Torre di Pisa

town la città

town hall il municipio

toy il giocattolo

toy store il negozio di giocattoli

tractor il trattore

tradition la tradizione

traffic il traffico

traffic jam l'ingorgo (m)

traffic lights il semaforo

trailer il rimorchio, la roulotte

train il treno

translate tradurre

translator il traduttore/la traduttrice

travel viaggiare

travel agent l'agenzia di viaggio (f)

traveler's check il travellers cheque

tray il vassoio

tree l'albero (m)

truck il camion

trunk (of car) il bagagliaio

true vero

try provare

Tuesday martedì

tunnel il tunnel

Turin Torino

turn: turn left/right giri a sinistra/destra

turn signal la freccia, l'indicatore di direzione (m)

Tuscany la Toscana

tweezers le pinzette

twelve dodici

twenty venti

twin room la camera a due letti

two due

typewriter la macchina da scrivere

U

ugly brutto

umbrella l'ombrello (m)

uncle lo zio

under ... sotto ...

underpants le mutande

underskirt la sottoveste

understand capire; *I don't understand* non capisco

underwear la biancheria intima

university l'università (f)

university professor il professore universitario/la professoressa universitaria

unleaded senza piombo

until fino a

unusual insolito

up su; (upward) verso l'alto; *up there* lassù

urgent urgente

us noi; *it's for us* è per noi

use l'uso (m); (verb) usare; *it's no use* non serve a niente

useful utile

usual solito

usually di solito

V

vacancy (room) la stanza libera

vacation la vacanza

vaccination la vaccinazione

valley la valle

valuables gli oggetti di valore

valve la valvola

vanilla la vaniglia

vase il vaso

Vatican il Vaticano; *Vatican City* la Città del Vaticano
VCR il videoregistratore
veal la carne di vitello
vegetables la verdura
vegetarian vegetariano
vehicle il veicolo
Venice Venezia
very molto; *very much* moltissimo
vest la canottiera
vet il veterinario
video (tape/film) il video cassetta; *video games* i videogiochi
view la vista
viewfinder il mirino
villa la villa
village il paese, il villaggio
violin il violino
visit la visita; (verb) andare a trovare
visitor (guest) l'ospite
vitamin pill la compressa di vitamine
vodka la vodka
voice la voce; *voicemail* la segreteria telefonica

W

wait aspettare; *wait!* aspetta!
waiter il cameriere
waiting room la sala d'aspetto
waitress la cameriera
Wales il Galles
walk la passeggiata; (verb) camminare; *to go for a walk* andare a fare una passeggiata
wall il muro
wallet il portafoglio
want volere; *I want* (io) voglio
war la guerra
wardrobe il guardaroba, l'armadio (m)
warm caldo
was: I was (io) ero; *he/she/it was* (lui/lei/esso) era
wash (verb) lavare
washing machine la lavatrice
wasp la vespa
watch l'orologio (m); (verb) guardare
water l'acqua (f)
water heater lo scaldabagno
waterfall la cascata
wave l'onda (f); (verb: with hand) salutare
wavy: wavy hair i capelli ondulati
we noi

weather il tempo
website il sito internet
wedding il matrimonio
Wednesday mercoledì
weed l'erbaccia (f)
week la settimana
welcome benvenuto; *you're welcome* di niente, prego
well done (food) ben cotta
Wellington boots gli stivali do gomma
Welsh gallese
Welshman il gallese
Welshwoman la gallese
were: you were (Lei) era; (singular, familiar) (tu) eri; (plural) (voi) eravate; *we were* (noi) eravamo; *they were* (loro) erano
west l'ovest (m)
wet bagnato
what? cosa?
wheel la ruota; *wheel brace* il girabacchino
wheelchair la sedia a rotelle
when? quando?
where? dove?; *where are you from?* di dov'è?/di dove sei? (formal/informal)
whether se
which? quale?
white bianco
who? chi?
why? perchè?
wide ampio
wife la moglie
wind il vento
window la finestra
windshield il parabrezza
wine il vino; *wine list* la lista dei vini; *wine shop* l'enoteca (f)
wing l'ala (f)
winter l'inverno (m)
with con
withdraw (money) prelevare
without senza
witness il/la testimone
woman la donna
wood (material) il legno
wool la lana
word la parola
work il lavoro; (verb) lavorare; (machine) funzionare
worry: don't worry non si preoccupi
worse peggiore
worst il peggiore
wrapping paper la carta da imballaggio; (for presents) la carta da regalo
wrench la chiave fissa
wrist il polso

writing paper la carta da scrivere
wrong sbagliato

X, Y, Z

X-ray la radiografia
year l'anno (m)
yellow giallo
yes sì
yesterday ieri
yet ancora; *not yet* non ancora
yield dare la precedenza
yogurt lo yogurt
you: (singular, formal) Lei; (singular, informal) tu; (plural) voi
young giovane
your: (singular, formal) *your book* il suo libro; *your shirt* la sua camicia; *your shoes* le sue scarpe; (singular, informal) *your book* il tuo libro; *your shirt* la tua camicia; *your shoes* le tue scarpe
yours: is this yours? (singular, formal) è suo?; (singular, informal) è tuo?
youth hostel l'ostello della gioventù (m)
zipper la chiusura lampo
zoo lo zoo

Dictionary
Italian *to English*

The gender of Italian nouns listed here is indicated by the abbreviations "(m)" and "(f)," for masculine and feminine. Plural nouns are followed by the abbreviations "(m pl)" or "(f pl)." Italian adjectives "(adj)" vary according to the gender and number of the word they describe, and the masculine form is shown here. In general, adjectives that end in **-o** adopt an **-a** ending in the feminine form, and those that end in **-e** usually stay the same. Plural endings are **-i** for masculine and **-e** for feminine.

A

a *in, at, per;* a casa *at home;* a Venezia *in Venice;* all'ufficio postale *at the post office;* alla stazione *to the station;* alle tre *at 3 o'clock;* a persona *per person;* all'anno *per annum*
abbastanza *enough, quite (fairly)*
abbronzarsi *to get a suntan*
abbronzato *suntanned*
acceleratore (m) *accelerator*
accendino (m) *lighter*
accensione (f) *ignition*
acqua (f) *water;* l'acqua di seltz *soda water;* l'acqua gassata *sparkling water;* l'acqua minerale *mineral water;* l'acqua naturale *still water;* l'acqua potabile *drinking water;* l'acqua tonica *tonic water*
acquazzone (m) *shower (rain)*
adesso *now*
aereo (m) *aircraft*
aeroporto (m) *airport*
affare (m) *business, bargain;* non sono affari tuoi *it's none of your business*
affittare *to rent*
affollato *crowded*
agenda (f) *planner*
agente immobiliare (m/f) *realtor*
agenzia di viaggio (f) *travel agent*
aglio (m) *garlic*
agnello (m) *lamb*
ago (m) *needle*
agosto *August*
agricoltore (m) *farmer*
Aids *AIDS*

aiuola (f) *flowerbed*
aiutare *to help*
aiuto (m) *help*
ala (f) *wing*
albero (m) *tree, mast;* l'albero a camme *camshaft*
albicocca (f) *apricot*
alcol (m) *alcohol*
alimentari (m pl) *grocery store*
alla salute! *cheers! (toast)*
allergico *allergic*
alloggio (m) *accommodation*
allora *then*
le Alpi *the Alps*
al sangue *rare (steak)*
alt! *stop!*
alto *high, tall*
altro *other;* l'altro *the other (one);* un altro, un'altra *another;* l'uno o l'altro *either of them;* un altro, per favore *same again, please;* qualcos'altro *something else;* qualcun'altro *someone else;* da qualche altra parte *somewhere else*
alzarsi *get up*
amare *to love*
amaro *bitter*
ambasciata (f) *embassy*
ambulanza (f) *ambulance*
America (f) *America*
americano *American*
amico/amica (m/f) *friend*
ammiratore (m) *fan (enthusiast)*
ampio *wide*
ampliamento (m) *enlargement*
ananas (m) *pineapple*
anche too *(also)*
ancora *yet;* non ancora *not yet*
andare *to go;* andare a trovare *to visit*

anello (m) *ring (jewelry)*
angolo (m) *corner*
animato *busy (bar)*
anniversario (m) *anniversary*
anno (m) *year*
anticipo (m) *advance (on payment, etc.);* anticipato *in advance*
antiquario (m) *antique shop*
antisettico (m) *antiseptic*
aperitivo (m) *aperitif*
aperto *open (adj)*
apparecchio acustico (m) *hearing aid*
appartamento (m) *apartment*
appetito (m) *appetite*
appuntamento (m) *appointment*
apribottiglie (m) *bottle opener*
aprile *April*
aprire *to open*
apriscatole (m) *can opener*
arachidi (m pl) *peanuts*
arancia (f) *orange (fruit)*
arancione *orange (color)*
arazzo (m) *tapestry*
architettura (f) *architecture*
argento (m) *silver (color);* d'argento *silver (metal)*
aria (f) *air*
aria condizionata (f) *air conditioning*
armadio (m) *cupboard, wardrobe*
arrivare *to arrive*
arrivederci *goodbye*
arrivi *arrivals*
arrossamento (m) *rash*
arrosto *roasted*
arte (f) *art*
articoli per la casa (m pl) *household products*
artista (m/f) *artist*

ascensore (m) *elevator*
asciugamano (m) *towel*
asciutto *dry*
asmatico *asthmatic*
asparagi (m) *asparagus*
aspettare *wait*; aspetta! *wait!*
aspirina (f) *aspirin*
assegno (m) *check*
assicurazione (f) *insurance*
assomiglia a ... *it's like ...*
assorbenti (igienici) (m pl) *sanitary napkins*
attaccapanni (m) *coat hanger*
attento *careful*; stia attento! *be careful!*
atterrare *to land*
attraente *attractive*
attraverso *through*
aula delle lezioni (f) *lecture hall*
auricolari (m pl) *earphones*
l'Australia (f) *Australia*
australiano *Australian*
autista (m/f) *driver* (of bus, truck, etc.)
auto (m) *car*
autobus (m) *bus*; la stazione degli autobus *bus station*; la fermata dell'autobus *bus stop*
automatico *automatic*
autostop: fare l'autostop *to hitchhike*
autostrada (f) *expressway*
autunno (m) *fall, autumn*
a vapore *steamed*
avere *to have*; non ho ... *I don't have ...*; ha ...?; *do you have ...?*
avvocato (m) *lawyer*
azienda turistica (f) *tourist informaion*
azzurro *blue*

B

babbo (m) *dad*
baffi (m pl) *mustache*
bagagli (m pl) *luggage*
bagagliaio (m) *trunk* (of car)
bagaglio a mano (m) *carry-on luggage*
bagaglio in eccesso (m) *excess baggage*
bagnato *wet*
bagno (m) *bathroom*; fare il bagno *to take a bath*; i bagni *restrooms*
balcone (m) *balcony*
ballare *to dance*
ballo (m) *dance*
balsamo (m) *conditioner* (hair)

bambino (m), bambina (f) *baby, child*
bambola (f) *doll*
banana (f) *banana*
banca (f) *bank*
bancomat (m) *ATM*
banconota (f) *banknote*
banda (f) *band* (music)
bandiera (f) *flag*
bar (m) *bar* (drinks)
barba (f) *beard*
barbiere (m) *barber*
barca (f) *boat* (small)
basso *low, short*
basta! *enough!*; basta così *that'll be all*
battello (m) *boat* (passenger)
batteria (f) *battery*
baule (m) *chest* (furniture)
beige *beige*
bello *beautiful, handsome, nice*
bene *good, well*; bene! *good!*; benissimo! *great!*; ben cotta *well done* (food); non mi sento bene *I don't feel well*; ti sta bene *it suits you*
benvenuto *welcome*
benzina (f) *gasoline*
benzinaio (m) *gas station*
bere *to drink*
berretto (m) *cap* (hat)
biancheria (f) *laundry* (dirty clothes)
biancheria intima (f) *underwear*
bianco *white*
bibita (f) *drink*
biblioteca (f) *library*
bicchiere (m) *glass* (for drinking)
bicicletta (f) *bicycle*
bigliettaio (m) *conductor* (bus)
biglietteria (f) *ticket office, booking office*
biglietto (m) *ticket, card*; il biglietto di andata e ritorno *round-trip ticket*; il biglietto di sola andata *one-way ticket*; il biglietto da visita (m) *business card*; il biglietto di auguri *greetings card*
bigodini (m pl) *curlers*
bikini (m) *bikini*
binario (m) *platform*
biondo *blond*
birra (f) *beer*
biscotto (m) *cookie*
bisogno (m) *need*; ho bisogno di ... *I need ...*; non c'è bisogno *there's no need*

bloc-notes (m) *notepad*
blu *navy blue*
bocca (f) *mouth*
boccaglio (m) *snorkel*
bollire *to boil* (water); (egg, etc.) far bollire
bollitore (m) *teakettle*
borsa (f) *bag*
borsaiolo (m) *pickpocket*
borsellino (m) *purse*
botteghino (m) *box office*
bottiglia (f) *bottle*
bottone (m) *button*
braccialetto (m) *bracelet*
braccio (m) *arm*
brandy (m) *brandy*
bravo *clever*
brioche (f) *croissant*
britannico *British*
bruciare *to burn*
bruciatura (f) *burn*
brutto *ugly*
budget (m) *budget*
bunker (m) *bunker* (golf)
buonanotte *good night*
buonasera *good evening*
buongiorno *good day, hello*
buono *good, nice* (to eat); a buon mercato *cheap*
burro (m) *butter*; il burro di cacao *lip balm*
busta (f) *envelope*

C

c'è ... *there is ...*; c'è ...? *is there ...?*
cabina telefonica (f) *telephone booth*
cacciavite (m) *screwdriver*
caffè (m) *coffee, café*; il caffè solubile *instant coffee*
calcio (m) *soccer* (game)
calcolatore (m) *calculator*
caldaia (f) *boiler*
caldo *hot, warm*; ho caldo *I feel hot*
calzamaglia (f) *tights* (wool)
calze (f pl) *stockings*
calzini (m pl) *socks*
calzolaio (m) *shoe repairer*
cambiare *to change* (money, trains)
cambiarsi *to change* (clothes)
cambio (m) *change* (money), *gear* (car); il (tasso di) cambio *exchange rate*
camera (f) *(bed)room*; la camera a due letti *twin room*; la camera

doppia *double room*; la camera singola *single room*

camera d'aria (f) *inner tube*

cameriera (f) *waitress, maid*

cameriere (m) *waiter*

camicetta (f) *blouse*

camicia (f) *shirt*; la camicia da notte *nightgown*

caminetto (m) *fireplace*

camion (m) *truck*

camminare *to walk*

campagna (f) *country* (not town)

campana (f) *bell* (church)

campanello (m) *bell* (door)

campeggio (m) *campground*

camper (m) *camper van*

campo (m) *field*

il Canada *Canada*

canadese *Canadian*

canale (m) *canal*

cancello (m) *gate*

candela (f) *candle, spark plug*

cane (m) *dog*

canoa (f) *canoe*

canottiera (f) *vest*

cantare *to sing*

cantina (f) *basement*

canzone (f) *song*

capelli (m pl) *hair*

capire *to understand*; non capisco *I don't understand*

capotto (m) *coat*

cappello (m) *hat*

caramella (f) *sweet*

carburatore (m) *carburetor*

caricabatterie (m) *charger*

carino *nice, pretty*

carne (f) *meat*

caro *expensive*

carota (f) *carrot*

carrello (m) *cart*

carrozzina (f) *baby carriage*

carta (f) *paper, card*; la carta (geografica) *map*; la carta assegni *debit card*; la carta d'imbarco *boarding card*; la carta da imballaggio *wrapping paper*; la carta da regalo *wrapping paper* (for presents); la carta da scrivere *writing paper*; la carta di credito *credit card*; la carta igienica *toilet paper*; le carte da gioco *playing cards*

cartello (m) *sign* (in station, etc.)

cartella (f) *briefcase*

cartolina (f) *postcard*

casa (f) *house, home*

cascata (f) *waterfall*

cassa (f) *checkout*

cassetta (f) *box* (of wood), *cassette*; la cassetta delle lettere *mailbox*

cassetto (m) *drawer*

cassettone (m) *chest of drawers*

cassiere (m) *cashier*

castello (m) *castle*

catenaccio (m) *bolt* (on door)

cattedrale (f) *cathedral*

cattivo *bad*

cattolico *Catholic*

cavalcavia (m) *overpass*

cavatappi (m) *corkscrew*

caviglia (f) *ankle*

cavolfiore (m) *cauliflower*

cavolo (m) *cabbage*

celibe *single* (unmarried)

cellulare (m) *cell phone*

cena (f) *supper, dinner*

cento *hundred*

centro (m) *center*; il centro città *downtown*

cerotto (m) *adhesive bandage*

certificato (m) *certificate*

certo *certainly*

cesoie (f pl) *shears*

cestello (m) *basket* (in supermarket)

cestino (m) *basket*

cetriolo (m) *cucumber*

check-in (m) *check-in*; lo sportello del check-in *check-in desk*; fare il check-in *to check in*

chewing gum (m) *chewing gum*

chi? *who?*

chiamare *to call*

chiaro *light* (not dark), *clear* (obvious)

chiave (f) *key*; la chiave fissa *tire iron, wrench*

chiesa (f) *church*

chilo (m) *kilo*

chilometro (m) *kilometer*

chiodo (m) *nail* (metal)

chitarra (f) *guitar*

chiudere *to close*; chiudere con il catenaccio *to bolt*

chiuso *closed*

chiusura lampo (f) *zipper*

ciao *hello, hi*

ciascuno *each*; venti euro ciascuno *twenty euros each*

cibo (m) *food*

cieco *blind* (cannot see)

cielo (m) *sky*

cifre (f pl) *figures*

ciliegia (f) *cherry*

cimitero (m) *cemetery*

cin cin! *cheers!* (toast)

cinema (m) *movie theater*

cinghia della ventola (f) *fan belt*

cinquanta *fifty*

cinque *five*

cintura (f) *belt*; la cintura di sicurezza *seat belt*

cioccolata (f) *chocolate*; la scatola di cioccolatini *box of chocolates*

ciotola (f) *bowl*; la ciotola del cane *dog bowl*

cipolla (f) *onion*

cipria (f) *powder* (cosmetic)

circa 16 *about 16*

ci sono *there are ...*; ci sono? *are there ...?*

città (f) *city, town*

ciuccio (m) *pacifier* (for baby)

clacson (m) *horn* (car)

classe (f) *class*

cliente (m) *client*

codice segreto (m) *PIN*

cofano (m) *hood* (car)

cognome (m) *last name*

coincidenza (f) *connection*

colazione (f) *breakfast*

colla (f) *glue*

collana (f) *necklace*

collant (m pl) *pantyhose*

collare (m) *collar* (for dog)

collega (m/f) *colleague*

colletto (m) *collar*

collezione (f) *collection* (stamps, etc.)

collina (f) *hill*

collo (m) *neck*

colore (m) *color*

coltello (m) *knife*

come *like*; come questo *like this one*

come? *how?, sorry?* (pardon); come si chiama/ti chiami? *what's your name?* (formal/informal); come si chiama? *what's it called?*

comignolo (m) *chimney*

cominciare *to start*

commedia (f) *play* (theater)

commerciante (m/f) *shopkeeper*

comodino (m) *nightstand*

compact disc (m) *CD*

compleanno (m)
birthday; buon
compleanno! *happy
birthday!*

completo (m) *suit*

complicato *complicated*

comprare *buy*

compressa (f) *tablet*; la
compressa di vitamine
vitamin pill

computer (m)
computer; il computer
portatile *laptop
(computer)*

con *with*

concerto (m) *concert*

conchiglia (f) *shell*

conferenza (f) *lecture,
conference*; la sala
conferenze *conference
room*

confine (m) *border*

congelatore (m) *freezer*

congratulazioni!
congratulations!

coniglio (m) *rabbit*

conoscere *to know
(person)*

consegna (f) *delivery*

consolato (m) *consulate*

consulente finanziario
(m/f) *financial
consultant*

contento *glad, happy*

conto (m) *check
(restaurant)*

contraccettivo (m)
contraceptive

contratto (m) *contract*

contro *against*

controllo (m) *test*

conversazione (f) *talk*

coperta (f) *blanket*

copriletto (m)
bedspread

corda (f) *rope, guy rope,
string* (guitar, etc.)

cordiale *friendly*

corno (m) *horn*
(animal)

corpo (m) *body*

correre *to run*

corridoio (m) *corridor*

corrispondente (m/f)
pen pal

corso (m) *course*
(educational)

corto *short*

cosa? *what?*; cosa c'è?
what's the matter

cosmetici (m pl)
cosmetics

costare *to cost* ; quanto
costa? *what does it
cost?*

costoletta (f) *chop* (food)

costoso *expensive*

costume da bagno (m)
*swimsuit, swimming
trunks*

cotone (m) *cotton*; il
cotone idrofilo *cotton
balls*

cozze (f pl) *mussels*

crampo (m) *cramp*

cravatta (f) *tie*

crema (f) *cream, lotion*

criceto (m) *hamster*

crociera (f) *cruise*

crostacei (m pl)
shellfish (crabs, etc..)

cucchiaio (m) *spoon*

cuccia (f) *dog basket*

cucina (f) *kitchen, stove*

cucinare *to cook*

cucire *to sew*

cucitrice (f) *stapler*

cugino/cugina *cousin*

cuocere (al forno) *to
bake*

cuoco/cuoca (m/f)
cook

cuoio (m) *leather*

cuore (m) *heart*; nel
cuore della notte *in
the middle of the night*

cuori (m pl) *hearts*
(cards)

curry (m) *curry*

cuscino (m) *cushion*

D

dado (m) *nut* (for bolt)

dappertutto *everywhere*

dare *to give*; dare la
precedenza *to yield*

davanti a *opposite, in
front of*

decollo (m) *takeoff*

deliberatamente
deliberately

denaro (m) *cash*

dente (m) *tooth*

dentiera (f) *dentures,
false teeth*

dentifricio (m)
toothpaste

dentista (m/f) *dentist*

denuncia (f) *statement*
(to police)

deodorante (m)
deodorant

desposito bagagli (m)
left luggage locker

dessert (m pl) *desserts*

destro *right* (not left)

detersivo (m)
detergent; il detersivo
(per bucato) *laundry
detergent*; il detersivo
per i piatti
dishwashing liquid

devo *I must*; devo
andare adesso *I must
go now*

di *of, from, than, on, at*:
più di *more than*; di
dov'è?/di dove sei?
where are you from?
(formal/informal);

di lunedì *on Monday*;
di notte *at night*

diabetico *diabetic*

diamante (m) *diamond*
(gem)

diarrea (f) *diarrhea*

dica? *can I help you?*

dicembre *December*

diciannove *nineteen*

diciassette *seventeen*

diciotto *eighteen*

dieci *ten*

dietro *behind*; dietro a
... *behind* ...

difficile *difficult*

dimenticare *to forget*

dire *to say*; che cosa ha
detto? *what did you
say?*; come si dice ...?
how do you say ...?

direttore (m) *conductor*
(orchestra)

direttore/direttrice
manager

direzione (f) *office*

dirigente (m) *executive*

disabili (m pl) *the
disabled*

discesa per principianti
(f) *beginners' slope*

disco (m) *record*
(music)

dito (m) *finger*

divano (m) *sofa*

diversi *several*

diverso; è diverso! *that's
different!*

divertente *funny*

divieto di accesso *no
entry*

divorziato *divorced*

dizionario (m)
dictionary

doccia (f) *shower*

docciaschiuma (f)
shower gel

documento (m)
document; il documento
d'identità *identification*

dodici *twelve*

dogana (f) *customs*

dolce *sweet* (not sour)

dollaro (m) *dollar*

dolore (m) *ache, pain*

domanda (f) *question*

domani *tomorrow*; a
domani *see you
tomorrow*

domenica *Sunday*

donna (f) *woman*;
la donna delle pulizie
cleaner

dopo *after*

dopobarba (m)
aftershave

dormire *to sleep*

dottore (m) *doctor*

dove? *where?*

due *two*; le due *two
o'clock*

dune (f pl) *sand dunes*

duomo (m) *cathedral*
durante *during*
duro *hard*
duty free (m) *duty-free*

E

e *and*; e poi? *what next?*
è *he/she/it is*
eccellente *excellent*
ecco *here you are, here it is*
economico *cheap*
edificio (m) *building*
elastico (m) *elastic, rubber band*
elettricista (m/f) *electrician*
elettricità (f) *electricity*
elettrico *electric*
email (f) *email*
emergenza (f) *emergency*
enoteca (f) *wine shop*
entrare *to enter*
entrata (f) *entrance*
entro (venerdì) *by (Friday)*
epilettico *epileptic*
equipaggio (m) *crew*
era: (Lei) era *you were* (singular, formal); (lui/lei/esso) era *he/she/it was*
erano *they were*
eravamo *we were*
eravate *you were* (plural)
erba (f) *grass*
erbaccia (f) *weed*
eri *you were* (singular, informal)
eritema solare (m) *sunburn*
ero *I was*
errore (m) *mistake*
esatto *right* (correct)
esaurimento nervoso (m) *nervous breakdown*
esca (f) *bait*
escursione (f) *excursion*
escursionismo (m) *hiking*
esempio (m) *example*; per esempio *for example*
esposimetro (m) *light meter*
esso *it*
est (m) *east*
estate (f) *summer*
estintore (m) *fire extinguisher*
etichetta (f) *label*

F

faccia (f) *face*
facile *easy*
fagioli (m pl) *beans*

falegname (m) *carpenter*
falò (m) *campfire*
fame: ho fame *I'm hungry*
famiglia (f) *family*
fantastico *fantastic*
fare *to do, to make*; che lavoro fa? *what (work) do you do?*
fare jogging *to jog*; andare a fare jogging *to go jogging*
fare la fila *to line up* (wait)
fari (m pl) *lights, headlights*; i fari posteriori *rear lights*
farina (f) *flour*
farmacia (f) *pharmacy*
fascia (f) *bandage*
fattore di protezione (m) *SPF (sun protection factor)*
fattoria (f) *farm*
fattura (f) *invoice*
favore: per favore *please*
fax (m) *fax, fax machine*; (verb: document) spedire via fax
fazzolettini di carta (m pl) *tissues*
febbraio *February*
febbre (f) *fever, temperature*
fegato (m) *liver*
felice *happy*
felpa (f) *sweatshirt*
ferita (f) *injury*
fermare *to stop* ; fermo! *stop!*
fermata dell'autobus (f) *bus stop*
ferramenta (f) *hardware store*
ferro (m) *iron* (metal); (for clothes) il ferro da stiro
ferrovia (f) *railroad*
festa (f) *party* (celebration)
fiammifero (m) *match* (light)
fidanzata (f) *fiancée*, (adj) *engaged*
fidanzato (m) *fiancé*, (adj) *engaged*
fiera (commerciale) (f) *fair* (trade)
figlia (f) *daughter*
figlio (m) *son*
fila (f) *line, aisle* (in supermarket, etc.)
filiale (f) *branch* (of company)
film (m) *film* (movies)
filtro (m) *filter*
finalmente! *at last!*
fine (f) *end*
finestra (f) *window*
finito *finished*

fino a *until*
finocchio (m) *fennel*
fiore (m) *flower*
fiori *clubs* (cards)
Firenze *Florence*
firmare *to sign*
fissare *to arrange* (appointments, etc)
fiume (m) *river*
flash (m) *flash* (camera)
flauto (m) *flute*
flebo (f) *intravenous drip*
foglia (f) *leaf*
fohn (m) *hair dryer*
fondo (m) *bottom*; in fondo (a) *at the bottom (of)*
foratura (f) *puncture*
forbici (f pl) *scissors*
forchetta (f) *fork* (for food)
foresta (f) *forest*
forestiero (m) *foreigner*
formaggio (m) *cheese*
forno (m) *oven*; il forno a microonde *microwave*
forse *maybe, perhaps*
forte *loud, strong*
fortuna (f) *luck*; buona fortuna! *good luck!*
fotocopiatrice (f) *photocopier*
fotografare *to photograph*
fotografia (f) *photograph*
fotografo (m) *photographer*
foulard (m) *headscarf*
fra ... *between ...*
fragola (f) *strawberry*
francese *French*
la Francia *France*
francobollo (m) *stamp*
fratello (m) *brother*
frattura (f) *fracture*
freccia (f) *turn signal*
freddo *cold* (adj)
frenare *to brake*
freno (m) *brake*; il freno a mano *hand brake*
fresco *cool*
fretta: ho fretta *I'm in a hurry*
friggere *to fry*
frigorifero (m) *refrigerator*
fritto *fried*
frizione (f) *clutch*
frizzante *fizzy*
frutta (f) *fruit*
frutti di mare (m pl) *seafood*
fucile (m) *gun* (rifle)
fumare *to smoke*
fumatori *smoking* (section); non fumatori *nonsmoking*

fumo (m) *smoke*

fungo (m) *mushroom*

funivia (f) *cable car*

funzionare *to work* (machine)

fuochi d'artificio (m pl) *fireworks*

fuoco (m) *fire*

fuori *outside*

furto (m) *burglary*

G

gabbia (f) *cage*

galleria (f) *balcony* (in theater); la galleria d'arte *art gallery*

il Galles *Wales*

gallese *Welsh*

gamba (f) *leg*

gambero (m) *crayfish*

garage (m) *garage*

garantire *to guarantee*

garanzia (f) *guarantee*

gas *gas, fuel;* il gas da campeggio *stove fuel;* il gas per accendini *lighter fuel*

gatto (m) *cat*

gay *gay* (homosexual)

gasolio (m) *diesel*

gel (m) *gel* (hair)

gelato (m) *ice cream*

gelo (m) *frost*

gemelli (m pl) *cufflinks*

genitori (m pl) *parents*

gennaio *January*

Genova *Genoa*

gente (f) *people*

la Germania *Germany*

ghiaccio (m) *ice*

già *already*

giacca (f) *jacket*

giallo *yellow*

giardiniere (m) *gardener*

giardino (m) *garden*

gin (m) *gin*

ginocchio (m) *knee*

giocare *to play*

giocattolo (m) *toy*

gioielliere (m) *jeweler* (shop)

giornalaio (m) *newsstand*

giornale (m) *newspaper*

giorno (m) *day;* il giorno festivo *public holiday*

giovane *young*

giovedì *Thursday*

girabacchino (m) *tire iron*

giri a sinistra/destra *turn left/right*

giro *tour*

giù *down*

giugno *June*

giusto *right* (correct); non è giusto *it's not fair*

gli *the* (m pl)

gocce (f pl) *drops*

gola (f) *throat*

golf (m) *golf*

golfista (m) *golfer*

gomito (m) *elbow*

gomma (f) *eraser, tire;* la gomma a terra *flat tire*

gonna (f) *skirt*

governo (m) *government*

grafico/grafica (m/f) *designer*

la Gran Bretagna *Great Britain*

granchio (m) *crab*

grande *big, large*

grande magazzino (m) *department store*

grasso (m) *fat;* fat (adj)

gratis *free* (no charge)

gratuito *free* (no charge)

grave *serious* (illness)

grazie *thank you/ thanks*

grazioso *pretty* (beautiful)

la Grecia *Greece*

greco *Greek*

gridare *to shout*

grigio *gray*

griglia (f) *grill;* alla griglia *grilled*

grondaia (f) *gutter*

grotta (f) *cave*

gruppo (m) *group*

guanciale (m) *pillow*

guanti (m pl) *gloves*

guardare *to watch*

guardaroba (m) *wardrobe*

guardia (f) *guard*

guasto *breakdown* (car)

guerra (f) *war*

guida (f) *guide, guidebook;* la guida telefonica *telephone directory*

guidare *to drive*

guidatore/guidatrice (m/f) *driver* (car)

guinzaglio (m) *leash* (for dog)

gusto (m) *flavor*

H

ha ...? *do you have ...?*

hamburger (m) *hamburger*

HIV positivo *HIV-positive*

ho ... *I have ...*

hobby (m) *hobby*

I

i *the* (m pl)

idraulico (m) *plumber*

ieri *yesterday*

il *the* (m)

imbarazzante *embarrassing*

imbianchino (m) *decorator*

immediatamente *immediately*

immondizie (f pl) *garbage*

imparare *to learn*

impermeabile (m) *raincoat*

impiegato/impiegata (m/f) *office worker*

importa: non importa *it doesn't matter*

impossibile *impossible*

imposta (f) *shutter* (window)

in *in, to:* in inglese *in English;* in Inghilterra *to England;* in mezzo alla piazza *in the middle of the square;* in centro *to the center;* in ritardo *delayed*

inalatore (m) *inhaler* (for asthma, etc.)

incendio (m) *fire* (blaze)

inchiostro (m) *ink*

incidente (m) *accident*

incinta *pregnant*

incluso *included*

incontro (m) *meeting, match* (sports)

incrocio (m) *intersection*

indicatore di direzione (m) *turn signal*

indigestione (f) *indigestion*

indirizzo (m) *address;* l'indirizzo di posta elettronica *email address*

indistinto *faint* (unclear)

infermiere/infermiera (m/f) *nurse*

infezione (f) *infection*

informatica (f) *information technology*

informazioni (f pl) *information*

infradito (m pl) *flipflops*

ingegneria (f) *engineering*

l'Inghilterra (f) *England*

inglese *English*

ingorgo (m) *traffic jam*

iniezione (f) *injection*

inizio (m) *start*

insalata (f) *salad*

insegna (f) *sign* (road, etc.)

insegnante (m/f) *teacher*

insegnare *to teach*

insettifugo (m) *insect repellent*

insetto (m) *insect*

insieme *together*

insolito *unusual*

insonnia (f) *insomnia*

intelligente *clever*

interessante *interesting*

internet (f) *Internet*

interpretare *interpret*

interprete (m/f) *interpreter*

interruttore (m) *switch*

interurbana *long-distance* (call)

intossicazione alimentare (f) *food poisoning*

inverno (m) *winter*

invito (m) *invitation*

io *I*

l'Irlanda (f) *Ireland*; l'Irlanda del Nord *Northern Ireland*

irlandese *Irish*

isola (f) *island*

Italia *Italy*

italiano *Italian*

J, K

jazz (m) *jazz*

jeans (m pl) *jeans*

jogging (m) *jogging*

krapfen (m) *doughnut*

L

la *the* (f)

là *there*

lacca per i capelli (f) *hairspray*

lacci (m pl) *laces* (of shoe)

ladro (m) *burglar, thief*

laggiù *over there*

lago (m) *lake*

lamette (f pl) *razor blades*

lampada (f) *lamp*; la lampada da studio *reading lamp*

lampadina (f) *light bulb*

lampone (m) *raspberry*

lana (f) *wool*

lassativo (m) *laxative*

lassù *up there*

lato (m) *side* (edge)

latte (m) *milk*; il latte detergente *skin cleanser*

latteria (f) *dairy*

latticini (m pl) *dairy products*

lattina (f) *can* (vessel)

lattuga (f) *lettuce*

laureato: sono laureato in ... *I have a degree in ...*

lavabo (m) *sink*

lavanderia (f) *laundry* (place); la lavanderia a secco *dry-cleaner*

lavandino (m) *sink, wash basin*

lavastoviglie (f) *dishwasher*

lavatrice (f) *washing machine*

lavello (m) *sink* (kitchen)

lavorare *to work*

lavorare a maglia *knit*

lavoro (m) *job, work*

le *the* (f pl)

lecca lecca (m) *lollipop*

legare *to tie*

legge (f) *law*

leggere *to read*

leggero *light* (not heavy)

legno (m) *wood* (material)

lei *she*

Lei *you* (singular, formal)

lente (f) *lens*; le lenti a contatto *contact lenses*; le lenti semi-rigide *gas-permeable lenses*

lento *slow*

lenzuola (f pl) *bed linen*

lenzuolo (m) *sheet*

lesso *boiled*

lettera (f) *letter*

letteratura (f) *literature*

lettino (m) *crib*

letto (m) *bed*

leva del cambio (f) *gear stick*

levata (f) *pickup* (postal)

lezione (f) *lesson*

libbra (f) *pound* (weight)

libero *free* (not occupied)

libero professionista *self-employed*

libreria (f) *bookstore*

libretto degli assegni (m) *checkbook*

libro (m) *book*

limetta per le unghie (f) *nailfile*

limonata (f) *lemonade*

limoncello (m) *lime* (fruit)

limone (m) *lemon*

limpido *clear* (water)

linea (f) *line* (telephone, etc.); la linea aerea (f) *airline*; la linea esterna *outside line*

lingua (f) *language, tongue*

liquido per lenti (m) *soaking solution* (for contact lenses)

liquore (m) *liqueur*

lisca (f) *fishbone*

litro (m) *liter*

livido (m) *bruise*

lo *the* (m)

località sciistica (f) *ski resort*

locomotiva (f) *engine* (train)

lontano *far*; è lontano? *is it far away?*

loro *they, their, them*; la loro stanza *their room*; il loro amico *their friend*; i loro libri *their books*; le loro penne *their pens*; è loro *it's theirs*; è per loro *it's for them*; dallo a loro *give it to them*

lozione solare (f) *suntan lotion*

lucchetto (m) *padlock*

luce (f) *light*

luci di posizione (f pl) *parking lights*

lucido per le scarpe (m) *shoe polish*

luglio *July*

lui *he, him*; è per lui *it's for him*

luna (f) *moon*; la luna di miele (f) *honeymoon*

luna park (m) *fair* (funfair)

lunedì *Monday*

lunghezza (f) *length*

lungo *long*

M

ma *but*

macchina (f) *car*

macchina da scrivere (f) *typewriter*

macchina fotografica (f) *camera*

macelleria (f) *butcher shop*

madre (f) *mother*

magari *perhaps*

maggio *May*

maglieria (f) *knitwear*

maglione (m) *sweater*

magro *thin*

mai *never*; non fumo mai *I never smoke*

mal di denti (m) *toothache*

mal di pancia (m) *stomachache*

mal di testa (m) *headache*

malato *ill*

male: mi fa male il/la ... *my ... hurts*; farà male? *will it hurt?*

mamma *mom*

mancia (f) *tip* (money)

mandare *to send*

mandarino (m) *tangerine*

mangianastri (m) *cassette player*

mangiare *to eat*

manica (f) *sleeve*

maniglia (f) *handle* (door)

mano (f) *hand*

manzo (m) *beef*

marciapiede (m) *sidewalk*

mare (m) *sea*

marea (f) *tide*

margarina (f) *margarine*

marito (m) *husband*

marmellata (f) *jam*; la marmellata d'arance *marmalade*

marmitta (f) *exhaust* (car)

marmo (m) *marble*

marrone *brown*

martedì *Tuesday*

martello (m) *hammer*

marzo *March*

mascara (m) *mascara*

materassino gonfiabile (m) *air mattress*

materasso (m) *mattress*

matita (f) *pencil*

matrimoniale (f) *double room*

matrimonio (m) *wedding*

mattina (f) *morning*; di mattina *in the morning*

maturo *ripe*

meccanico (m) *mechanic*

medicina (f) *medicine*

medico (m) *doctor*

il Mediterraneo *the Mediterranean*

medusa (f) *jellyfish*

mela (f) *apple*

melone (m) *melon*

meno *less*

menta piperita (f) *peppermint*

menù (m) *menu*

mercato (m) *market*

mercoledì *Wednesday*

mese (m) *month*

messa (f) *mass* (church)

messaggio (m) *message*

metà *half*

metro(politana) (f) *subway, metro*

mettere *to put*

mezzanotte *midnight*

mezzo (f) *half*: ... e mezzo *half past ...*; mezz'ora *half an hour*; mezzo pensione *half-board*

mezzogiorno *noon*

mia *my*; la mia borsa *my bag*

mi chiamo... *my name is ...*

mi dispiace *I'm sorry*

mie *my*; le mie chiavi *my keys*

miei *my*; i miei vestiti *my dresses*

miele (m) *honey*

migliore (m) *best, better*; migliore di *better than*

Milano *Milan*

milione *million*

mille *thousand*

minestra (f) *soup*

minuto (m) *minute*

mio *my, mine*; il mio libro *my book*; è mio *it's mine*

mirino (m) *viewfinder*

mi scusi! *excuse me!* (to get attention)

mobili (m pl) *furniture*

moda (f) *fashion*

modem (m) *modem*

modulo per la domanda (m) *application form*

moglie (f) *wife*

molla (f) *spring* (mechanical)

molletta (f) *clothespin*

molluschi (m pl) *shellfish* (mollusks)

molo (m) *dock*

molto *a lot*; molto meglio *much better*; molto più lentamente *much slower*; non molto *not much*

moltissimo *very much*

moneta (f) *coin*

monitor (m) *monitor* (computer)

montagna (f) *mountain*

monumento (m) *monument*

mora (f) *blackberry*

morbido *soft*

mordere *bite* (verb: by dog)

morire *to die*

morso (m) *bite* (noun: by dog)

morto *dead*

mosaico (m) *mosaic*

mosca (f) *fly* (insect)

mostra (f) *exhibition*

motocicletta (f) *motorcycle*

motore (m) *engine* (car)

motorino (m) *moped*

motoscafo (m) *motorboat*

mountain bike (m) *mountain bike*

mouse (m) *mouse* (computer)

municipio (m) *town hall*

muovere *to move*; non muoverti! *don't move!*

muratore (m) *builder, handyman*

muro (m) *wall*

museo (m) *museum*

musica (f) *music*; la musica classica *classical music*; la musica folk *folk music*; la musica pop *pop music*

musicista (m) *musician*

mutande (f pl) *underpants*

N

Napoli *Naples*

naso (m) *nose*

Natale (m) *Christmas*

nato: sono nato nel 1975 *I was born in 1975*

nave (f) *boat, ship*; la nave a vapore *steamer* (boat)

nebbia (f) *fog*

necessario *necessary*

negativa (f) *negative* (photo); (adj) *negativo*

negozio (m) *store, shop*; il negozio di dischi *record store*; il negozio di giocattoli (m) *toy store*

neozelandese (m/f) *New Zealander*; (adj) *New Zealand*

nero *black*

nessuno *nobody*; da nessuna parte *nowhere*

neve (f) *snow*

niente *nothing*; di niente *you're welcome*; non serve a niente *it's no use*

night (m) *nightclub*

nipote (f) *granddaughter, niece*

nipote (m) *grandson, nephew*

no *no* (negative response)

nocciola (f) *nut*

noce (f) *nut*

noi *we, us*; è per noi *it's for us*

noioso *boring*; che noia! *that's boring!*

noleggiare *to rent*

nome (m) *name*; il nome di battesimo *first name*

non *not*; non è ... *he's not ...*

nonna (f) *grandmother*

nonni (m pl) *grandparents*

nonno (m) *grandfather*

nord (m) *north*

normale *ordinary*

nostro/a *our*; il nostro albergo *our hotel*; la nostra macchina *our car*; è nostro *it's ours*

notizie (f pl) *news*; (on radio) il notiziario

notte (f) *night*

novanta *ninety*

nove *nine*

novembre *November*

nubile *single* (unmarried: woman)

numero (m) *number, shoe size*; il numero di telefono *telephone number*

nuotare *to swim*

nuoto (m) *swimming*

la Nuova Zelanda *New Zealand*

nuovo *new*; di nuovo *again*

O

o *or*; o ... o ... *either ... or ...*

obbligatorio *necessary*

occhiali (m pl) *glasses*

occhiali da sole (m pl) *sunglasses*

occhio (m) *eye*; gli occhi *eyes*

occupato *busy, occupied*

odore (m) *smell*

oggetti di valore (m pl) *valuables*

oggi *today*

ogni *each, every*; ogni tanto *occasionally*

ognuno *everyone*

olio (m) *oil*; olio d'oliva (m) *olive oil*

oliva (f) *olive*

ombrello (m) *umbrella*

ombrellone (m) *sunshade*

omelette (f) *omelet*

omeopatia *homeopathy*

omosessuale *gay (homosexual)*

onda (f) *wave*; i capelli ondulati (m pl) *wavy hair*

onesto *honest*

opera (f) *work (of art), opera*

operatore/operatrice (m/f) *operator*

operazione (f) *operation*

opuscolo (m) *brochure*

ora (f) *hour*; ora sono occupato *I'm busy now*

orario (m) *schedule, timetable*; l'orario di apertura *opening times*; l'orario di visita (m) *visiting hours*

orchestra (f) *orchestra*

ordinativo (m) *order (for goods)*

ordine del giorno (m) *agenda*

ore: che ore sono? *what's the time?*

orecchini (m pl) *earrings*

orecchio (m) *ear*; le orecchie *ears*

organo (m) *organ (music)*

oro (m) *gold*

orologio (m) *clock, watch*

orribile *awful, horrible*

ospedale (m) *hospital*

ospite (m/f) *guest*

ossigenare *to bleach (hair)*

osso (m) *bone*

ostello della gioventù (m) *youth hostel*

ottanta *eighty*

ottico (m) *optician*

ottimo *excellent*

otto *eight*

ottobre *October*

otturatore (m) *shutter (camera)*

otturazione (f) *filling (in tooth)*

ovest (m) *west*

P

pacchetto (m) *package, packet*

pacco (m) *parcel*

padella (f) *frying pan*

Padova *Padua*

padre (m) *father*

padrona di casa (f) *hostess*

padrone di casa (m) *host*

paese (m) *country (state), village*

pagamento (m) *payment*

pagare *to pay*; pagare in contanti *to pay cash*

pagina (f) *page*

paio (m) *pair*

palazzo (m) *palace*

palestra (f) *gymnastics*

palla (f) *ball (soccer, etc.)*

pallido *pale*

pallina (f) *ball (tennis, etc.)*

pallone (m) *ball, soccer ball*

palo della tenda (m) *tent pole*

pancetta (f) *bacon*

pane (m) *bread*; il pane tostato (m) *toast*

panetteria (f) *bread shop*

panino (m) *sandwich*; *rock (music)*

panna (f) *cream (dairy)*

pannolini (m pl) *diapers*

pantaloncini corti (m pl) *shorts*

pantaloni (m pl) *pants, trousers*

pantofole (m pl) *slippers*

papà (m) *dad*

Papa: il Papa *Pope*

parabrezza (m) *windshield*

paraffina (f) *kerosene*

paralume (m) *lampshade*

paraurti (m) *bumper*

parcheggiare *to park*

parcheggio (m) *parking lot*

parco (m) *park*

parlare *to talk, speak*; parla ...? *do you speak ...?*; non parlo ... *I don't speak ...*

parola (f) *word*

parrucchiere (m) *hair salon*

parte posteriore (f) *back (not front)*

partenza (f) *departure*; le partenze *departures*

particolarmente *especially*

partire *to depart, leave*

partito (m) *party (political)*

passaporto (m) *passport*; il controllo passaporti *passport control*

passatempo (m) *hobby*

passeggero/passeggera (m/f) *passenger*

passeggiata (f) *walk*; andare a fare una passeggiata *to go for a walk*

passegino (m) *pushchair*

password (f) *password*

pasta (f) *pasta*

pasticceria (f) *bakery*

pasticche per la gola (f pl) *throat lozenges*

pasto (m) *meal*

patata (f) *potato*

patatine (f pl) *chips*

patatine fritte (f pl) *french fries*

patente (f) *license*; patente di guida *driver's license*

patio (m) *terrace*

pattini da ghiaccio (m pl) *ice skates*

pattumiera (f) *garbage can*

paura: ho paura *I'm frightened*

pavimento (m) *floor (ground)*

pazzo *crazy*

pedone (m) *pedestrian*; la zona pedonale *pedestrian zone*

peggiore *worst, worse*

pelle (f) *leather*

pelletteria (f) *leather goods shop*

pellicola (f) *film (for camera)*

penicillina (f) *penicillin*

penna (f) *pen*

pennello (m) *paintbrush*

pensare *to think*; penso di sì *I think so*; ci penserò *I'll think about it*

pensione completa (f) *full board*

pentola (f) *saucepan*; la pentola a pressione *steamer* (for cooking)

pepe (m) *pepper* (spice)

peperone (m) *pepper* (red, green)

per *for*; per me *for me*

pera (f) *pear*

perché *because*

perché? *why?, what for?*

perfetto *perfect*

pericoloso *dangerous*

periferia (f) *suburbs*

perla (f) *pearl*

permanente (f) *perm*

permesso *allowed*; permesso! *excuse me!* (to get past)

persiane (f pl) *shutters* (window)

pesante *heavy*

pesca (f) *peach, fishing*; andare a pesca *to go fishing*

pesce (m) *fish*

pescheria (f) *fishmonger (shop)*

pettinare *to comb*

pettine (m) *comb*

petto (m) *chest* (part of body)

pezzi di ricambio (m pl) *spare parts* (car)

pezzo (m) *piece*

piace: mi piace ... *I like ...*; mi piace nuotare *I like swimming*

piacere *pleased to meet you*

piacere di conoscerla *how do you do?*

piangere *cry* (verb: weep)

piano (m) *floor* (story); piano di lavoro *countertop*

pianta (f) *map* (of town), *plan*; *plant*

pianterreno (m) *ground floor*

piastrella (f) *tile*

piattino (m) *saucer*

piatto (m) *plate, meal*; i piatti pronti *prepared meals*

piatto *flat* (level)

piazza (f) *square*

piazzola (f) *site* (in campground, etc.)

picche (m pl) *spades* (cards)

picchetto (m) *tent peg*

piccolo *little, small*

picnic (m) *picnic*

piede (m) *foot*; a piedi *on foot*

pieno *full*

pigiama (m) *pajamas*

pigro *lazy*

pin (m) *PIN*

pinacoteca (f) *art gallery*

pinne (f pl) *flippers*

pinzette (f pl) *tweezers*

pioggia (f) *rain*

piovra (f) *octopus*

pipa (f) *pipe* (for smoking)

piscina (f) *swimming pool*

piselli (m pl) *peas*

pistola (f) *gun* (pistol)

pistone (m) *piston*

pittura (f) *painting*

più *more*; più di ... *more than ...*; più presto possibile *as soon as possible*

piumino (m) *comforter*

piuttosto *pretty, quite*

pizzo (m) *lace*

plastica (f) *plastic*

platea (f) *orchestra* (in theater)

po' *a little*; è un po' grande *it's a little big*; solo un po' *just a little*

poi *then*

polipo (m) *octopus*

politica (f) *politics*

polizia (f) *police*

poliziotto (m) *police officer*

pollame (m) *poultry*

pollo (m) *chicken*

polso (m) *wrist*

poltrona (f) *armchair*

pomata (f) *ointment*

pomeriggio (m) *afternoon*

pomodoro (m) *tomato*

ponte (m) *bridge*

porcellana (f) *china*

porta (f) *door*

portacenere (m) *ashtray*

portafoglio (m) *wallet*

portare *to bring*; da portare via *to carry out*

portiere (m) *porter* (hotel); il portiere di notte *night porter*

portinaio/portinaia *caretaker*

porto (m) *harbor, port*

possibile *possible*

posso avere ...? *can I have ...?*

posta (f) *mail*; la posta elettronica *email*

posteggio dei taxi (m) *taxi stand*

postino (m) *mail carrier*

posto (m) *place, accommodation, seat*

postumi della sbornia (m pl) *hangover*

potreste ...? *can you ...?*

povero *poor*

pranzo (m) *lunch*

prato (m) *lawn*

preferire *to prefer*

prego *you're welcome*; prego? *pardon?*

prelevare *to withdraw* (money)

prendere *to fetch* (something)

prendere *to take*; prendere il sole *to sunbathe*; prendere il treno *to catch the train*

prenotare *to book*

prenotazione (f) *reservation*

preoccupi: non si preoccupi *don't worry*

presa di corrente (f) *electrical hookup*

preservativo (m) *condom*

presto *early*; a presto *see you soon*

prete (m) *priest*

preventivo (m) *estimate*

prezzemolo (m) *parsley*

prezzo (m) *price*; il prezzo d'ingresso *admission charge*

prima di ... *before ...*

primavera (f) *spring* (season)

primi piatti (m pl) *appetizers*

primo *first*; il primo piano *second floor*; la prima classe *first class*

principiante (m/f) *beginner*

privato *private*

problema (m) *problem*; non c'è problema *no problem*

professore/professoressa (m/f) *teacher*; il professore universitario *university lecturer*

profitti (m pl) *profits*

profondo *deep*

profumo (m) *perfume*

proibito *forbidden*

prolunga (f) *extension cord*

pronto *ready, hello* (on phone)

pronto soccorso (m) *emergency department, first aid*

prosciutto (m) *ham*

prossimo *next*; la settimana prossima *next week*

provare *to try*

pubblico *public*

pulce (f) *flea*

pulire *to clean*

pulito *clean* (adj)

pullman (m) *long-distance bus*

pungere *to bite* (by insect)

punta (f) *tip* (end)

puntina da disegno (f) *thumbtack*

puntura (f) *bite* (by insect)

può *he/she can*; non può ... *he/she can't ...*

puzzare *to smell* (stink)

Q

quaderno (m) *notebook*

quadrato *square* (adj: shape)

quadri (m pl) *diamonds* (cards)

qualche modo *somehow*

qualche parte *somewhere*

qualche volta *sometimes*

qualcosa *something*

qualcuno *somebody*

quale? *which?*

qualità (f) *quality*

quando? *when?*

quant'è? *how much is that?*

quanti anni hai? *how old are you?*

quanto ci vuole? *how long does it take?*

quanto costa? *how much?*

quanto dista da qui ...? *how far is it to ...?*

quaranta *forty*

quarto (m) *quarter*; ... e un quarto *quarter past ...*

quarto *fourth*

quasi *almost*

quattordici *fourteen*

quattro *four*

quei *those*; quei ragazzi *those boys*

quella *that*; quella donna *that woman*

quelle *those*; quelle cose *those things*

quelli *those*; prendo quelli *I'll take those*

quello *that*; quell'uomo *that man*; cos'è quello? *what's that?*

questa *this*; questa donna *this woman*

queste *these*; queste cose *these things*

questi *these*; questi ragazzi *these boys*

questo *this*; questo quadro *this picture*; quest'uomo *this man*; cos'è questo? *what's this?*; questo è il signor ... *this is Mr ...*

quindici *fifteen*

R

raccomandata *registered* (mail)

radersi *to shave*

radiatore (m) *radiator*

radio (f) *radio*

radiografia (f) *X-ray*

raffreddore (m) *cold* (illness); ho un raffreddore *I have a cold*

ragazza (f) *girl*

ragazzo (m) *boy*

ragioniere/ragioniera (m/f) *accountant*

ragno (m) *spider*

rapporto di polizia (m) *police report*

raro *rare* (uncommon)

rastrello (m) *rake*

ratto (m) *rat*

ravanello (m) *radish*

reception (f) *reception* (hotel)

receptionist (m/f) *receptionist*

record (m) *record* (sports, etc.)

regalo (m) *gift*

reggiseno (m) *bra*

relazione (f) *report*

religione (f) *religion*

remare *to row*

remi (m pl) *oars*

rene (m) *kidney*

reparto (m) *department, ward*; il reparto di pediatria *children's ward*

respirare *to breathe*

resti (m pl) *ruins*

restituire *to return* (give back)

resto (m) *rest* (noun: remainder)

reticella (per i bagagli) (f) *luggage rack*

riavere indietro qualcosa *to get something back*

ribes nero (m) *black currant*

ricci (m pl) *curls*

ricco *rich*

ricerca (f) *research*

ricetta (f) *prescription*

ricevere *to get* (obtain)

ricevuta (f) *receipt* (restaurants, hotels)

ricordare *to remember*; non ricordo *I don't remember*

ridere *to laugh*

riduttore (m) *adapter*

riduzione (f) *discount*

rifiuti (m pl) *litter* (trash can)

riga (f) *ruler* (for drawing)

rilassarsi *to relax*

rimorchio (m) *trailer*

rinfreschi (m pl) *refreshments*

rinfresco *reception* (party)

ringraziare *to thank*

riparare *to repair*

ripieno (m) *filling* (in sandwich, cake, etc.)

riposarsi *to rest*

riscaldamento (m) *heating*; il riscaldamento centrale *central heating*

riscuotere *to cash*

riso (m) *rice*

ristorante (m) *restaurant*

ritardo: l'autobus è in ritardo *the bus is late*

ritiro bagagli (m) *baggage claim*

ritornare *to return*

riunione (f) *meeting*

rivista (f) *magazine*

roccia *rock* (stone)

Roma *Rome*

romanzo (m) *novel*

rosa (f) *rose*; *pink* (color)

rossetto (m) *lipstick*

rosso *red*

rotatoria (f) *roundabout*

rotondo *round* (circular)

rotto *broken*; la gamba rotta *broken leg*

roulotte (f) *trailer, camper trailer*

rovine (f pl) *ruins*

rubare *steal*; è stato rubato *it's been stolen*

rubinetto (m) *tap*

rubino (m) *ruby* (gem)

rugby (m) *rugby*

rullino a colori (m) *color film*

rum (m) *rum*

rumoroso *noisy*

ruota (f) *wheel*

ruscello (m) *stream*

S

sabato *Saturday*

sabbia (f) *sand*

sacchetto (m) *bag*; il sacchetto di plastica (m) *plastic bag*; il sacchetto per la pattumiera (m) *garbage bag*

sacco a pelo (m) *sleeping bag*

sala (f) *room*; la sala d'aspetto *waiting room*; la sala da pranzo *dining room*; la sala operatoria *operating room*

salame (m) *salami*

saldi (m pl) *sale (at reduced prices)*

sale (m) *salt*

salire *to go up*; salire su *to get on* (bus, etc.)

salmone (m) *salmon*

salsa (f) *sauce*

salsiccia (f) *sausage*

salumeria (f) *delicatessen*

salutare *to wave*

sandali (m pl) *sandals*

sangue (m) *blood*; le analisi del sangue *blood test*

sapere *know (fact)*; I don't know non so

sapone (m) *soap*

la Sardegna *Sardinia*

sauna (f) *sauna*

sazio *full (up)*: sono sazio *I'm full (after a meal)*

sbagliato *wrong*

sbrigati! *hurry up!*

scacchi (m pl) *chess*

scala (f) *staircase*; le scale *stairs*; la scala mobile *escalator*

scaldabagno (m) *water heater*

scambiare *to exchange*

scarpe (f pl) *shoes*; le scarpe da ginnastica *athletic shoes*

scatola (f) *box, tin*

scendere *to go down*; scendere da *to get off* (bus, etc.)

scheda telefonica (f) *phonecard*

schermo (m) *screen*

scherzo (m) *joke*

schiena (f) *back (body)*

schiuma (f) *foam, mousse, cream (for hair)*; la schiuma da barba *shaving cream*

sci (m pl) *skis*

scialle (m) *shawl*

sciare: andare a sciare *to go skiing*

sciarpa (f) *scarf*

scienza (f) *science*

sciroppo (m) *syrup*

scodella (f) *bowl*

scompartimento (m) *compartment*

scontrino (m) *receipt (shops, bars)*

scopa (f) *brush (cleaning)*

la Scozia *Scotland*

scozzese *Scottish*

scritto da ... *written by ...*

scrivania (f) *desk*

scuola (f) *school*

scuro *dark*

scusate! *excuse me! (when sneezing, etc.)*

scusi! *sorry!*; scusi? *pardon?*

se *if, whether*

secchio (m) *bucket*

secco *dry* (wine)

secondi piatti (m pl) *main courses*

secondo *second*; seconda classe *second class*

sede centrale (f) *headquarters*

sedia (f) *chair*; la sedia girevole *swivel chair*; la sedia a rotelle *wheelchair*

sedici *sixteen*

seggiolino per macchina (m) *car seat (for a baby)*

segretario/segretaria (m/f) *secretary*; la segreteria telefonica *answering machine*; la segreteria telefonica *voicemail*

sei *six*

sei *you are* (singular, informal)

semaforo (m) *traffic lights*

seminario (m) *seminar*

seminterrato (m) *basement*

semplice *simple*

sempre *always*; sempre dritto *straight ahead*

senape (f) *mustard*

senso unico *one way*

sentiero (m) *path*

sentire *to hear*

senza *without*; senza piombo *unleaded*

separati *separated (couple)*

separato *separate* (adj)

sera (f) *evening*

serio *serious*

servizio in camera (m) *room service*

sessanta *sixty*

seta (f) *silk*

sete *thirsty*; ho sete *I'm thirsty*

settanta *seventy*

sette *seven*

settembre *September*

settimana (f) *week*; la settimana scorsa *last week*

shampoo (m) *shampoo*

sherry (m) *sherry*

shopping *shopping*

short (m pl) *shorts*

sì *yes*

sia ... che ... *both ... and ...*

siamo *we are*

la Sicilia *Sicily*

sicuro *safe (not dangerous)*; *sure (certain)*; sei sicuro? *are you sure?*

siepe (f) *hedge*

siete *you are* (plural, informal)

sigaretta (f) *cigarette*

sigaro (m) *cigar*

significa: che cosa significa? *what does this mean?*

Signor *Mr.*

signora (f) *lady, madam*; Signora *Mrs.*

signore *sir*

Signorina *Miss*

simpatico *nice* (pleasant)

sinagoga (f) *synagogue*

sinistra *left (not right)*

sito internet (m) *website*

slittare *to skid*

smalto per le unghie (m) *nail polish*

soffitta (f) *attic*

soffitto (m) *ceiling*

soffocante *stuffy*

soggiorno (m) *living room*

soldi (m pl) *money*

sole (m) *sun*; c'è il sole *it's sunny*

solito *usual*; di solito *usually*

sollievo: che sollievo! *what a relief!*

solo *alone, single (one), only*; da solo *by oneself*

sonnifero (m) *sleeping pill*

sonno (m) *sleep*

sono *I am*; sono di ... *I come from ...*

sopra *over (above)*

sopracciglio (m) *eyebrow*

sordo *deaf*

sorella (f) *sister*

sorpassare *to pass (driving)*

sorridere *to smile*

sorriso (m) *smile*

sosta vietata *no parking*

sotto *below, under*

sottoveste (f) *underskirt*

souvenir (m) *souvenir*

la Spagna *Spain*

spagnolo *Spanish*

spago (m) *string (cord)*

spalla (f) *shoulder*

spazio (m) *room (space)*

spazzatura (f) *garbage*

spazzola (f) *hairbrush*

spazzolare *to brush (hair)*

spazzolino da denti (m) *toothbrush*

specchio (m) *mirror*

spedire per posta *to mail*

spesa (f) *shopping*; andare a fare la spesa *to go shopping*

spesso *often*; *thick*

spettatori *audience*

spiacente *I'm sorry*

spiaggia (f) *beach*

spicci (m pl) *cash, change*

spilla (f) *brooch*; la spilla di sicurezza *safety pin*

spillatrice (f) *stapler*

spina *plug* (electrical)

spinaci (m pl) *spinach*

spingere *to push*

sporco *dirty*

sport (m) *sports*

sportello (m) *door* (of car); lo sportello automatico *ATM*

sposato *married*

spuntino (m) *snack*

stampante (f) *printer*

stampelle (f pl) *crutches*

stanco *tired*

stanza (f) *room*; stanza libera *vacancy* (room)

star (f) *star* (film)

stasera *tonight*

statua (f) *statue*

stazione (f) *station*; la stazione di polizia *police station*; la stazione di servizio (f) *gas station*

steccato (m) *fence*

stella (f) *star*

stereo (m) *music system*

sterlina (f) *pounds sterling*

stesso *same*; lo stesso vestito *the same dress*

stirare *to iron*

stivale (m) *boot* (footwear); gli stivali do gomma *Wellington boots*

stoffa (f) *fabric*

stomaco (m) *stomach*

storia (f) *history*

straccio per la polvere (m) *duster*

strada (f) *road, street*

straniero (m) *foreigner*

strano *odd, funny*

stretta di mano (f) *handshake*

stretto *narrow, tight* (clothes)

strofinaccio (m) *dishcloth*

strumento musicale (m) *musical instrument*

studente/studentessa (m/f) *student*

stupido *stupid*

su *on, over* (above); sul tavolo *on the table*; un libro su Venezia *a book on Venice*

succo (m) *juice*; il succo d'arancia *orange juice*; il succo di frutta *fruit juice*; il succo di pomodoro *tomato juice*

sud (m) *south*

sudare *to sweat*

sudore (m) *sweat*

suo *her/his/your* (singular, formal): il suo libro *her/his/ your book*; la sua casa *her/his/your house*; le sue scarpe *her/his/your shoes*; i suoi vestiti *her/his/ your dresses*; è suo *it's hers/his/yours*

suoceri (m pl) *in-laws*

supermercato (m) *supermarket*

supplemento *supplement*

supposta (f) *suppository*

surgelati (m pl) *frozen foods*

sveglia (f) *alarm clock*

svenire *to faint*

sviluppare *to develop* (film)

la Svizzera *Switzerland*

svizzero *Swiss*

T

tabaccaio (m) *tobacconist's (shop)*

tabacco (m) *tobacco*

tacco (m) *heel* (of shoe)

taglia (f) *size* (clothes)

tagliare *to cut, chop*

tagliaunghie (m) *nail clippers*

taglio (m) *cut, haircut*

talco (m) *talcum powder*

tallone (m) *heel* (of foot)

tamponi (m pl) *tampons*

tappeto (m) *carpet, rug*

tappo (m) *cap* (bottle), *cork, plug* (sink)

tardi *late*; si sta facendo tardi *it's getting late*; più tardi *later*

targa (f) *license plate*

tariffa (f) *fare, rate*; la tariffa ridotta (f) *discount rate*

tasca (f) *pocket*

tastare *to feel* (touch)

tastiera (f) *keyboard*

tavoletta di cioccolata (f) *bar of chocolate*

tavolo (m) *table*

taxi (m) *taxi*

tazza (f) *cup*

tazzone (m) *mug*

tè (m) *tea*; il tè con latte *tea with milk*

teatro (m) *theater*

tecnico (m) *technician*

tedesco *German*

telefonare *to telephone*

telefonata (f) *telephone call*

telefonino (m) *cell phone*

telefono (m) *telephone*

televisione (f) *television*

telo protettivo (m) *flysheet*

telone impermeabile (m) *groundsheet*

temperamatite (m) *pencil sharpener*

temperatura (f) *temperature*

temperino (m) *penknife*

tempesta (f) *storm*

tempo (m) *time, weather*; il tempo libero *leisure time*

temporale (m) *thunderstorm*

tenda (f) *curtain, tent*; la tenda avvolgibile *blind* (on window)

tennis (m) *tennis*

terminale (m) *terminal* (airport)

termosifone (m) *heater*

terra (f) *soil, land*

terribile *awful, terrible*

terrina (f) *mixing bowl*

terzo *third*

testa (f) *head*

testimone (m/f) *witness*

tetto (m) *roof*

il Tevere *the Tiber*

tirare *to pull*

tisana (f) *herbal tea*

toilette (f) *toilet*; (men's room) la toilette degli uomini; (ladies' room) la toilette delle donne

topo (m) *mouse* (animal)

torcia (elettrica) (f) *flashlight*

Torino *Turin*

tornare *to come back*

torre (f) *tower*

torta (f) *cake*

tosaerba (m) *lawnmower*

la Toscana *Tuscany*

tosse (f) *cough*

tossire *to cough*

tovagliolo (m) *napkin*

tradizione (f) *tradition*

tradurre *to translate*

traduttore/traduttrice (m/f) *translator*

traffico (m) *traffic*

traghetto (m) *ferry*

trampolino (m) *diving board*

tranquillo *quiet*

traslocare *to move* (to new house)

trattore (m) *tractor*

tre *three*
trecento *three hundred*
tredici *thirteen*
treno (m) *train*
trenta *thirty*
triste *sad*
troppo *too* (excessively)
trucco (m) *makeup*
tu *you* (singular, informal)
tubo (m) *hose, pipe* (for water)
tuffarsi *to dive*
tuffo (m) *dive* (noun
tunnel (m) *tunnel*
tuo *your* (singular, informal); il tuo libro *your book*; la tua camicia *your shirt*; le tue scarpe *your shoes*; è tuo? *is this yours?*
turista (m/f) *tourist*
tutto *all*; tutto *everything*; tutte le strade *all the streets*; questo è tutto *that's all*; tutti *everyone*; tutti i giorni *every day*
TV cavo *cable TV*
TV satellite *satellite TV*

U

ubriaco *drunk*
uccello (m) *bird*
udire *to hear*
ufficio (m) *office*; l'ufficio oggetti smarriti *lost property office*; l'ufficio postale *post office*; l'ufficio turistico *tourist office*
ultimo *last* (final)
umido *damp*
un/uno/una/un' *a*
undici *eleven*
unghia (f) *nail* (finger)
unguento (m) *ointment*
università (f) *university*
uno *one*; l'una *one o'clock*
uomo (m) *man*; gli uomini *men*
uovo (m) *egg*
urgente *urgent*
usare *to use*
uscire *to go out*
uscita (f) *exit, gate* (at airport)
uso (m) *use*
utile *useful*
uva (f) *grapes*
uvetta (f) *raisins*

V

vacanza (f) *vacation*
vaccinazione (f) *vaccination*
vagone letto (m) *sleeper car*
valigia (f) *case, suitcase*

valle (f) *valley*
valvola (f) *valve*
vanga (f) *spade* (shovel)
vaniglia (f) *vanilla*
varecchina (f) *bleach*
vasca (f) *bathtub*
vaso (m) *vase*
vassoio (m) *tray*
vattene! *go away!*
il Vaticano *Vatican*; la Città del Vaticano *Vatican City*
vecchio *old*
vedere *to see*
vegetariano *vegetarian*
veicolo (m) *vehicle*
vela (f) *sailing*
veleno (m) *poison*
veloce *fast, quick*
velocità (f) *speed*
vendere *to sell*
vendite (f pl) *sales* (of goods, etc.)
venerdì *Friday*
Venezia *Venice*
venga qui! *come here!* (informal); venga con me *come with me* (informal)
venire *to come*
venti *twenty*
ventilatore (m) *fan* (ventilator)
vento (m) *wind*
verde *green*
verdura (f) *vegetables*
vernice (f) *paint*
vero *true*
vespa (f) *wasp*
vestito (m) *dress*; i vestiti *clothes*
veterinario (m) *vet*
vetro (m) *glass* (material)
via aerea *air mail*
viaggiare *to travel*
viaggio (m) jtrip, journey
viale (m) *driveway*
vialetto (m) *path*
vieni qui! *come here!* (formal); vieni con me *come with me* (formal)
vicino (a) *close, near* (to); vicino alla finestra *near the window*; vicino alla porta *near the door*
video cassetta (m) *video* (tape/film)
videogiochi (m pl) *video games*
videoregistratore (m) *VCR*
villa (f) *villa*
villaggio (m) *village*
vino (m) *wine*; la lista dei vini *wine list*
viola *purple*
violino (m) *violin*

visita (f) *visit*; la visita guidata *guided tour*
vista (f) *view*
vita (f) *life, screw*
vivaio (m) *garden center*
vocabolarietto (m) *phrasebook*
voce (f) *voice*
vodka (f) *vodka*
voi *you* (plural)
volantino (m) *leaflet*
volare *to fly*
volere *to want*
volo (m) *flight*; il numero del volo *flight number*
vorrei *I'd like*
vuoto *empty*

W, Y, Z

whisky (m) *whisky*
yogurt (m) *yogurt*
zaino (m) *backpack*
zanzara (f) *mosquito*
zenzero (m) *ginger* (spice)
zia (f) *aunt*
zio (m) *uncle*
zoo (m) *zoo*
zucchero (m) *sugar*
zuppa (f) *soup*

Acknowledgments

The publisher would like to thank the following for their help in the preparation of this book: Fiorella Elviri and Anna Mazzotti for the organization of location photography in Italy; Farmacia Gaoni, Rome; La Taverna dei Borgia, Rome; Treni Italia, Tuscolana, Rome; Coolhurst Tennis Club, London; Magnet Showroom, Enfield, MyHotel, London; Kathy Gammon; Juliette Meeus and Harry.

Language content for Dorling Kindersley by G-AND-W PUBLISHING
Managed by **Jane Wightwick**
Editing and additional input: **Paula Tite**

Additional design assistance: **Lee Riches, Fehmi Cömert, Sally Geeve**
Additional editorial assistance: **Paul Docherty, Nikki Sims, Lynn Bresler**
Picture research: **Louise Thomas**

Picture credits

Key:
t=top; b=bottom; l=left, r=right; c=center A=above; B=below

p2 Alamy RF: *Medioimages; p4/5* DK Images: *Max Alexander trl Demetrio Carrasco bl; p6/7* **Laura Knox:** *cl; p10/11* Alamy RF: *BananaStock cAr; RubberBall cBl, bl;* Ingram Image Library: *bl; p12/13* Alamy RF: *John Foxx cl, cAr; RubberBall br;* DK Images: *Steve Shott cBr;* Ingram Image Library: *tr, cr; p14/15* Alamy RF: *Comstock Images tcr; Think Stock bcl;* Ingram Image Library: *cAl, cl, cBl, cAr, cBr, bcr; p16/17* Alamy RF: *Think Stock crA;* Getty: *Taxi / James Day bcr;* Ingram Image Library: *tr; p18/19* DK Images: *David Murray tr; p22/23* DK Images: *cl, Andy Crawford cAr; Susanna Price br; Magnus Rew tcrB;* Ingram Image Library: *bcl, tcr; p24/25* DK Images: *clA, Dave King tcr; p26/27* Ingram Image Library: *cl; p28/29* DK Images: *John Bulmer tcr; Dave King cr; Matthew Ward bclA;* Ingram Image Library: *bcrA, bcr; p30/31* Alamy RF: *Comstock Images bcl;* DK Images: *cl; p32/33* DK Images: *bcl, bcr; Magnus Rew cl;* Ingram Image Library: *bl; p38/39* Alamy RF: *Imageshop / Zefa Visual Media cl; p40/41* DK: *Sean Hunter cl; p42/43* DK: *Demetrio Carrasco cAAr; Mike Dunning tcr; p44/45* Courtesy of Renault:: *c; p46/47* Alamy RF: *Imageshop / Zefa Visual Media br;* DK Images: *Sean Hunter bcl;* Ingram Image Library: *tclB; Courtesy of Renault:: tcr; p48/49* Alamy: *CuboImages cAl;* DK Images: *Max Alexander bcl; Kim Sayer c, cl; p50/51* Alamy: *Robert Harding Picture Library tr; Peter Titmuss cr; p52/53* Alamy RF: *Image Farm Inc cAr;* DK Images: *cl; p54/55* Alamy: *Frank Herholdt bcl; Jackson Smith cBl;* Alamy RF: *BananaStock cl; John Foxx c; Image Source cAr;* Ingram Image Library: *bl; Andy Crawford bclA; p56/57* Alamy: *CuboImages tcll;* DK Images: *Max Alexander clAA; Kim Sayer cAl, c; Courtesy of Renault:: bc; p58/59* Alamy: *Michael Juno tcr;* Alamy RF: *Brand X Pictures cBl, cBBl; Image Source cAAl;* DK Images: *cAl; p60/61* Alamy: *Robert Harding Picture Library bcr;* Alamy RF: *Image Source cAr; Barry Mason bl;* DK Images: *Steve Gorton tcrB; Pia Tryde cAAr;* Ingram Image Library: *cr; p62/63* DK Images: *Stephen Whitehorn c; p64/65* Alamy: *Arcaid bcrA;* Alamy RF: *GKPhotography cBr; Goodshoot cAAr; Justin Kase tcrB;* DK Images: *Roger Moss c; Steve Tanner cAr;* Ingram Image Library: *cr; p66/67* Alamy: *Arcaid tl;* Alamy RF: *Image Source cAr;* DK Images: *tr; Stephen Whitehorn bl;* Ingram Image Library: *br; p68/69* Alamy: *Balearic Pictures cr; p72/73* Alamy RF: *imagebroker tcrB; Image Source cAr; Comstock Images tcr;* Avery Weight-Tronix: *bl; p74/75* Alamy RF: *Doug Norman bl;* Ingram Image Library: *cr; p76/77* Alamy: *Balearic Pictures cAl;* Momentum Creative Group cAl; Shoosh / Up the Res cBl;* Ingram Image Library: *cl; p84/85* Alamy: *Brand X Pictures cr; f1 Online c;* Alamy RF: *BananaStock bl; SuperStock tr;* Ingram Image Library: *crB; p86/87* Alamy RF: *Luca DiCecco bcl;* Getty: *Taxi / Rob Melnychuk tc; p90/91* Alamy RF: *Brand X Pictures tcr;* DK Images: *cl; David Jordan cAr; Stephen Oliver cr;* Ingram Image Library: *cBr; p82/93* Alamy RF: *Pixland cr;* DK Images: *cl Guy Ryecart tr; p94/95* Alamy: *David Kamm cl; Phototake Inc bcl;* Alamy RF: *Comstock Images cr; ImageState Royalty Free br;* DK Images: *Stephen Oliver tcr; p96/97* Alamy RF: *Pixland br;* DK Images: *tl;* Ingram Image Library: *tr; p98/99* Alamy: *Shotfile cr;* Alamy RF: *Bildagentur Franz Waldhaeusl bl; Keith Levit c; ThinkStock br; p100/101* DK Images: *Steve Gorton tcr; p102/103* Alamy: *Hortus b; D Hurst tcrB;* Alamy RF: *image100 tcr;* DK Images: *Geoff Brightling cAAr;* Ingram Image Library: *cAr; p104/105* DK Images: *Paul Bricknell cl(6); Jane Burton bcl; Geoff Dann cl(2); Max Gibbs cl(4); Frank Greenaway cl(3); Dave King cl(1), cAr; Tracy Morgan c(5); p106/107* DK Images: *Shotfile cr;* DK Images: *Geoff Brightling br; p110/111* Alamy RF: *RubberBall cr;* DK Images: *Andy Crawford cl; p112/113* Alamy RF: *BananaStock tr; Image Source bl;* DK Images: *cl;* Ingram Image Library: *bcrA; p114/115* Alamy: *FogStock tcr;* Alamy RF: *Image Source cAr; Index Stock bcl; p116/117* Alamy RF: *image100 cAl; p118/119* Alamy RF: *Pixland tcr;* GettyNews: *Giuseppe Cacace c; p120/121* Alamy: *ImageState / Pictor International c;* Alamy RF: *Sarkis Images tcr;* DK Images: *cBl, bcl; p122/123* Alamy RF: *BananaStock cA;* Ingram Image Library: *cl; p124/125* Alamy: *ImageState / Pictor International bcl;* DK Images: *cBl, bcl; Paul Bricknell tc(5); Geoff Dann tc(3); Max Gibbs tc(1); Frank Greenaway tc(2); Dave King tc(4); Tracy Morgan tc(6); p126/127* Alamy RF: *Image Farm Inc bl; p128* DK Images: *Neil Mersh.*

All other images **Mike Good.**